There is no other performer quite like Gloria Estefan. In the fast-paced music business where artists come and go with each passing year, she has sustained her success now for over fifteen years. Gloria and Miami Sound Machine have sold ten million albums, many of which have gone gold or multi-platinum, and racked up nine Top Ten hit singles.

In concert, Gloria is a magical presence, dazzling audiences with her Latinized pop music. When she takes the stage, whether in the U.S., Europe, Latin America, or at home in Miami, she builds her audience into an unequaled frenzy of excitement.

In a very real way, Gloria Estefan has changed the face of contemporary pop music.

—*from the Introduction*

Gloria Estefan

GRACE CATALANO

PRODUCED BY LAMPPOST PRESS

ST. MARTIN'S PAPERBACKS

GLORIA ESTEFAN

Copyright © 1991 by Grace Catalano and Lamppost Press.

Cover photo by Ilpo Musto/L.F.I.

ISBN: 0-312-92586-7

Printed in the United States of America

St. Martin's Paperbacks edition/May 1991

10 9 8 7 6 5 4 3 2 1

To Joey and Phillip
for the inspiration . . .

Contents

Introduction

If Gloria Estefan didn't exist, a writer might have had to invent her. For Gloria's story, a classic rags-to-riches fairy tale, is begging to be told.

Throughout her life, this energetic performer has been a fighter, never afraid to accept a challenge. Her story begins in Havana, Cuba, where she was born, and continues in Miami, Florida, where she grew up. Gloria's life has been peppered with happiness and tragedy.

From her humble beginnings, Gloria Estefan, a shy young girl, has become a superstar in the world of music. But not before overcoming almost impossible odds and surviving several major setbacks. Her story should be an inspiration to everyone.

The lithe, beautiful singer with the smoldering almond-shaped eyes and tangle of long, dark hair has been performing with Miami Sound Machine for over fifteen years. But, as a child, she had no real desire to become a professional singer. Opportunity presented itself as if by destiny. Music, to Gloria, was a means of escaping the daily pressures of watching her father deteriorate from multiple sclerosis, a disease doctors attributed to the Agent Orange poisoning he was exposed to in Vietnam.

From the time she was eleven years old until she was sixteen, Gloria took care of him every day after school. Because she was shy, she learned to sing and play the guitar locked in her room. "I contained everything within myself," she says. "I was very introverted, and could only let myself go when I sang in my room."

Later, she would muster up enough nerve to sing at parties with her cousin Merci. She was eighteen when Emilio Estefan, leader of a small party band known as the Miami Latin Boys, heard her and talked her into joining the group. Three years later, he asked her to marry him.

Though Gloria explains she was forced into the spotlight, she adds, "I'm a perfectionist and once I was there, it was, do it right or get out."

Gloria, of course, did it right—*very* right. She not only sang the group's songs, but also wrote many of them. And she helped Miami Sound Machine grow from a local Miami party band to a huge international success. Still, their climb to the top was gradual; it would take nine years before the world would be humming their songs.

If you didn't live in Miami, Florida, or follow the pop music scene in Europe and Latin America in the mid-seventies and early eighties, you probably didn't hear of Gloria Estefan or Miami Sound Machine. At that time, they recorded all their music in Spanish. It was only after they took a chance and released a song in English that they broke into the American pop market. The song that introduced Miami Sound Machine to the United States was the 1984 hit "Dr. Beat."

Since then, a string of dance hits and ballads have followed, beginning with "Conga," a song that cracked the pop, dance, black, and Latin charts simultaneously. Along the way, Gloria has gained more and more recognition as a singer and a songwriter.

The bulk of Miami Sound Machine's hits (in both English and Spanish) were either fully composed or cowritten by Gloria. They include "Words Get in the Way," "Rhythm Is Gonna Get You," "1-2-3," "Don't Wanna Lose You," "Oye Mi Canto," and "Anything for You," which came in number nine on the Top Ten Singles Chart for 1988.

In concert, Gloria is a magical presence, dazzling audiences with her Latin-tinged pop music. When she takes the stage, whether in the U.S., Europe, Latin America, or at home in Miami, she builds her audience into an unequaled frenzy of excitement.

There is no other performer quite like Gloria Estefan. In the fast-paced music business where artists come and go with each passing year, she has sustained her success now for over fifteen years. Gloria and Miami Sound Machine have sold 10 million albums, many of which have gone gold or multiplatinum, and racked up nine Top Ten hit singles.

In a very real way, she has changed the face of pop music since hitting it big in the late eighties. By mixing salsa with pop, Gloria and Miami Sound Machine built a bridge between Latin and American music. They opened some doors and made it a little easier for others to cross over.

David Glew, president of Epic Records, says of Gloria, "Besides Michael Jackson, she's one of our biggest and most important artists."

As Gloria Estefan celebrated her thirty-third birthday on September 1, 1990, surrounded by the people she loved most in the world, she had good reasons for her immeasurable joy. Only six months before, her strength and courage had been put to the test. She was on tour, promoting her lastest album, *Cuts Both Ways.* The tour had already been interrupted once before in December, when a blood vessel in her throat ruptured, requiring two months of rest. Gloria was in perfect health and excellent physical shape when she decided to resume touring on March 7.

But she had only played a few dates when, once again, the tour was canceled. This time it was for more serious reasons. On the snowy day of March 10, Gloria was involved in a near-fatal accident when the tour bus she was traveling in with her husband, son, and three others crashed en route to a concert date in Syracuse. Gloria broke a vertebra in her middle back that required delicate spinal surgery and a year of convalescence. In one split second, all that she worked for could have been gone. But somehow, she knew that wouldn't happen.

"I tried to lift my legs," Gloria said later, "but they would only go so far. I told Emilio I broke my back, but he tried to reassure me, saying, 'No baby, maybe you just pulled a muscle.' But I could feel it. I remember thinking I would rather die than be paralyzed. I told myself, 'No way, I'm not accepting this.' "

Lying on the floor of the bus, holding the hand of her young son, everything suddenly flashed before her. "How everything can change from one second to the next," she thought. All the memories of her life came rushing back—the pained childhood, the images of her father, the early years with Emilio when he performed with the band, building up Miami Sound Machine's reputation. Now Gloria had come face-to-face with one more obstacle.

But Gloria would write her own ending to the accident that almost left her paralyzed. And her ending would be a happy one. She had already been through a series of stormy times in her life, but always managed to rise above them.

Gloria Estefan traveled a long way to get where she is today. Nothing ever stopped her from achieving her goals and nothing ever will. She is sure of that.

This is her remarkable story.

 1

Stranded in a New Homeland

Cuba was already in turmoil when Gloria Maria Fajardo was born in Havana on September 1, 1957. Her father, Jose Manuel, had been a Cuban soldier, motorcycle escort to the former President Fulgencio Batista, and Pan American volleyball medalist. Her mother, Gloria, was a schoolteacher who when she was young had dreamed of going to Hollywood. In the 1940s, she won an international contest to dub Shirley Temple's movies into Spanish. But her father wouldn't let her leave Havana for Hollywood, so those dreams never became reality.

When Gloria was just sixteen months old, her father took his young family and fled to Miami to escape Fidel Castro's regime. Only ninety miles across the water, they were hoping, like so many others, to find freedom. Torn from the life and the world they knew, they arrived in Miami penniless and unwanted.

"We were part of the first wave of Cubans in Miami," explains Gloria. "When my mother first went to look for an apartment, it was a case of 'No children, no pets, no Cubans.'"

Because she was so young when she left Cuba, Gloria has very little recollection of life there. Her first real memories are of her early childhood in Miami and how tough it was for all Cubans in this new homeland. "There was a lot of prejudice. All these Hispanics were coming into one place that had never had any Hispanics before," she says.

The huge influx of Cubans put tremendous strain on the housing capacity of a city that was unprepared to accommodate such a large group. Every day more families from Cuba arrived in Miami and the apartment buildings had to quickly learn to cope with this swollen population. Sometimes as many as ten to fifteen members of one family lived in the same few rooms. They stayed close together because very few spoke English. By remaining a group, it was easier for them to communicate.

Gloria's parents rented a small apartment in the Cuban ghetto behind the Orange Bowl. Soon after, Jose was recruited for the 2506 Brigades, the CIA-funded band of Cuban refugees who were eventually sent on the failed Bay of Pigs invasion. A determined man, Jose believed in freedom and fighting for it. Gloria remembers, "Freedom was the most important thing to my father. I'll always remember him as being very idealistic. He was the head of the Tanks Division. When they unloaded the tanks at Bay of Pigs, he was leading the invasion."

The anti-Castro exiles landed the invasion force in southern Cuba on April 17, 1961. Many of the invaders were killed and twelve hundred were captured. Gloria's father was captured by his own cousin and went to jail.

For a year and a half, he was imprisoned in Cuba, along with hundreds of others. It was a traumatic period in the Cuban exile community. Gloria remembers, "All the men were gone, all the mothers and kids were living together."

During that time, she and her mother survived in the rundown apartment complex they nicknamed the Barracks. It was a place where newspapers were used as bed sheets and dinner was served from tin cans. It was also the place where Gloria's early musical talents were brought out.

Gloria was a bright light in these bleak times. It was apparent to everyone that this dark-haired, brown-eyed little girl was someone quite special. Even as a young child, Gloria's smile could charm neighbors and friends and lift their spirits. In the apartment complex, she soon became everyone's favorite.

Because her father was away for so much of her young life, her grandmother and mother would play the most important roles in shaping Gloria's future. She credits both of them with introducing her to music. She was an extremely shy, sensitive, and impressionable child, who learned the words to all the songs her mother sang.

Gloria's mother encouraged her to sing for the other women whose husbands were also imprisoned, to help alleviate their harsh living conditions. As their sole source of entertainment, Gloria would try to cheer them up. But her music was only a reminder of a life they had known and lost. As they congregated to listen, tears would well up in their eyes.

Gloria was too young at the time to know why her music moved the group to tears instead of applause, but now she understands.

"After a few verses, they would cry," she explains. "To them, the music was saying, 'When I left Cuba, I left my heart. I left my life. When I left Cuba, I left my heart buried there.' So I guess that could make them cry, especially because of what they'd just been through. Now I understand, years later, why they cried all the time, but as a child it was hard."

For Gloria and her family, things would only get tougher. In 1963, President John F. Kennedy negotiated the release of captured prisoners in a trade for drugs and medicine. Gloria's father was freed, but he wasn't ready to settle down to a quiet life in Miami. He felt his duty was to continue fighting, and so he joined the United States Army. By fighting for the U.S., he hoped that someday America would return the favor and help him and other exiles liberate Cuba.

He would find out later that this wasn't meant to be. But for now, he moved his wife and daughter to Texas where he was stationed. While the family was living in Texas, Gloria's sister, Rebecca, was born. The family was transferred to South Carolina, where Jose volunteered for Vietnam, after he had earned his captain's bars.

While her father was overseas, Gloria, a

self-described "Army brat," made friends with children whose fathers were also in the army. Despite all the difficulties inherent in moving again, Gloria adjusted easily.

She was both physically active and bookish; one minute she'd be outside playing sports with the other kids, the next she'd be diligently studying by herself. Books always interested her and she did exceptionally well in school. She learned and mastered the English language quickly and maintained a straight-A average in all school subjects from first grade through high school and college.

One thing she always managed to avoid was boredom. Even on weekends, Gloria found things to keep herself busy.

It helped that Gloria's home life was pleasant. She had all the advantages her mother could afford. She enjoyed going to the movies and often accompanied her mother to the theater. It was a way for both of them to forget what was happening in Vietnam. The news was filled with war stories and Gloria's mother thought about her husband constantly. The images on the big screen provided a great escape.

But Gloria soon discovered another means of escape. It was at this time that she began listening to popular music. The biggest influence on her would be the songs of the British bands. "I had been exposed to many different kinds of music," she says. For example, she can remember getting goose bumps the first time she heard the sentimental ballad "Ferry Across the Mersey" by Gerry and the Pacemakers.

Ironically, Gloria would not be introduced to the rhythms of Latin music for quite a few years. Instead, she kept her transistor radio blasting the Top Forty. Like many other youngsters growing up during the middle sixties, British musicians like the Beatles, the Rolling Stones, and Peter and Gordon quickly became favorites. She'd sing along to the songs and borrow records from friends so she didn't have to wait to hear them on radio. Listening to popular music was Gloria's number-one love.

Gloria spent many hours with her younger sister, Rebecca. It was an idyllic time that should have lasted. After all, they had already been through so much trying to rebuild their lives in a new country. Unfortunately, tragedy loomed over the Fajardo family, a tragedy that would ultimately introduce Gloria to something she was not prepared for.

After two years in Vietnam, her father returned home. It was time, at last, to become a real family. In 1968, they moved back to Miami and tried to pick up the pieces of their lives. For Gloria, it was a time to reacquaint herself with her father. He had missed out on two years of her life and she wanted to fill him in on everything that had happened.

But there was something different about her father. Gloria had sensed a change in him ever since he returned from Vietnam. So had her mother, though neither spoke of it. But it was something they wouldn't be able to ignore for long.

He wasn't as strong as he had been. He didn't talk about reclaiming Cuba anymore. But then again, Gloria told herself, no one else did, either.

When the Fajardo family returned to Miami, they returned to a different place. The more than six hundred thousand Cubans who had come to Miami temporarily were now ready to begin new lives in America. Gloria belonged to the group dubbed "the one-and-a-half generation," meaning born in Cuba, raised in the United States. She lived in a section of town that was eventually renamed Little Havana or *Calle Ocho*.

This was now her home, the home of her mother, father, and sister. And they were happy to be there. Gloria never thought about going back to Cuba, though she says today it's still on the minds of many older people. "They always harbor a hope," she says. "But you have to realize how they feel. If you lived in a country until you were sixty-five years old, and all of a sudden they come and tell you the house that you've lived in is no longer your house, it belongs to the government, and then you have to leave and go to some other place where you don't speak the language, the thing that's going to be the strongest to you are those memories of your country."

Those feelings Gloria talks about today are the same feelings her father had back in the early 1960s. His desire had always been to return to the country where he was born and raised. But after Vietnam, Gloria remembers, those feelings were gone. He just seemed tired—too tired to talk, to get up out of bed in the morning, to walk up a flight of stairs. Gloria wondered what had happened to her father's enormous energy.

He seemed weak and, as each day progressed, he grew weaker. Then the warning signs started occurring. "He'd fall for no reason," says Gloria. "Or he'd stop for a red light, but the light would be green."

Gloria's mother decided to take her husband to the hospital for tests. She feared something was seriously wrong with him, for he was not the man she had known. His strength had suddenly vanished; he complained of numbing pains and had to be helped every time he stood up.

The diagnosis was shocking: multiple sclerosis. Later they found out he had been exposed to Agent Orange poisoning in Vietnam.

The unthinkable had happened. No one wanted to believe it. But the doctor's eyes were dull and sad when he informed Gloria's mother that Jose would eventually be restricted to a wheelchair and then a bed. His condition would only get worse.

Gloria's mother had tears rolling down her face as she listened to the doctor. But Gloria would not cry. Shaking her head in disbelief, she couldn't understand how this had happened to a man who had been so healthy. He had fought both at the Bay of Pigs and in Vietnam and spent time in jail as a prisoner of war, and it didn't seem fair that he wouldn't be able to lead a vital life.

When Jose returned home, he was already walking with a cane. The impact of that image is one Gloria describes as the "most unforgettable" in her life. It was love and pain and futility in one desolate moment. To see her father, who had been such a strong and physical person, unable to walk on his own was unbearable for her.

As her mother wrapped a loving arm around his waist and ushered him into the living room, Jose went over to Gloria. She looked up at him and smiled but he could see the hurt in her eyes. "Don't worry, Glorita, it will be all right," her father whispered. But it was a wish that never materialized. As the doctor predicted, his condition gradually deteriorated.

It would take time for Gloria to accept what had happened to her father. At eleven years of age, her entire world had fallen apart and she could not contain the sadness she felt. The next stage of young Gloria's life was devastating. Music was the only thing that could bring her the happiness she deserved.

 **2**

An Escape Route

Nothing in Gloria's childhood affected her as deeply as learning to cope with her father's illness. For the next five years, from the age of eleven to sixteen, Gloria would be responsible for taking care of him every day after school. With her father's condition slowly worsening, Gloria's mother became the family's sole supporter.

She worked days, trying to earn enough money to pay the bills. At night, she went back to school to study English and revalidate her Cuban teaching credentials. Gloria would help her mother learn the words of their new language, when it got too difficult.

Gloria's mother was a strong woman who ruled her family with a firm but loving hand.

From the beginning, she wanted to give her daughters the best opportunities. She tried to make sure Gloria and her sister Rebecca had as normal and happy childhoods as possible. But that was not so easy.

She had to depend on her oldest child more than she wanted to. Maintaining good grades is usually enough to fill the days of every child, but young Gloria also found herself nursing her father, taking care of her sister, and combining homework with many household chores.

Her mother was not a strict disciplinarian, but she did explain the importance of education to her daughters. Both Gloria and Rebecca would get the best education available, and they were taught to take advantage of every opportunity that came their way.

Luckily for Gloria, learning came easily. At school she was an honor student, attentive and eager to absorb knowledge. But her mother and teachers also noticed that she was withdrawn, serious, and excruciatingly shy. The older she got, the more introspective she became.

Gloria does not like to dwell on this period in her life; she rarely talks about her father and what his illness did to her. At a very young age, she was witnessing firsthand something most kids never have to see. When the school bell rang at the end of the day, Gloria's classmates would be free. She would watch as her class broke off into individual groups of friends. Some would stay in the gym and join various sports teams; others would venture to stores where they'd buy magazines and the latest 45 rpm records. Gloria would go home to her father.

There were days when she wished she could just be a regular kid like everyone else, but her father needed her constantly and she wasn't about to let him down. By the time she was thirteen, he was confined to his bed and virtually helpless. Day after day, he seemed to rely on Gloria's help more.

"My father knew I was there for him," she says. "But he was ashamed, embarrassed. Because sometimes I would have to clean him up."

With no one to talk to, Gloria felt really alone for the first time in her life. "I was in a situation that I could see no way of getting out of," she says. "I had to find a meaning in my life. I had to really go inside to find some kind of anchor for my life and for my own psyche and well-being. I had to find something that would keep me sane. It was a very difficult thing to see my father slowly deteriorating like that."

The teenage Gloria carried an enormous burden and sought to escape from it. The depression she was suffering from could have driven her to take drastic measures. If she had not been so strong, she may have wanted to end it all.

Though Gloria never had suicidal thoughts, it's a subject she reflects on honestly. "They say statistically that teenage suicides are very, very prevalent. A lot of people don't understand it, but I can understand it," she told one reporter.

The anchor she sought to find so desperately had been there all the time. Soon, Gloria turned her full attention to music. It was a logical choice since she had always been surrounded by music: her mother's family boasted several musicians and singers. Relatives on her father's side played different instruments. Still, Gloria had never fully felt the importance of music before. The melodies and lyrics would become her escape.

"It was a way for me to let out all my emotions and all my frustrations," she says. "Music would help me with all the things I was feeling, the sadness in my life. It was my release from everything. I would lock myself up in my room with my guitar for hours and just sing by myself. I wouldn't cry; I refused to cry. I was afraid if I let go just a little bit, it would all go. My guitar and singing was my way of crying."

At first, Gloria would pick up her guitar and strum it to comfort herself, to help her forget how sick her father was. Rather than succumbing to the depression she felt, she'd practice. She taught herself to play by reading songbooks she took out of the library regularly. Slowly, music began to shape Gloria's entire world.

Now, when she came home from school, she had something to look forward to. She would attend to her father's and sister's needs, then go into her room and pluck on the taut strings of her guitar.

Within a short time, Gloria went from playing notes to chords to melodies. Then she began to sing by playing along with pop songs. Music gave Gloria pleasure and she pursued it with a deep sense of gratitude. She would sing "for fun and for emotional catharsis." She had a natural ear and couldn't forget a melody if she tried. Tunes ran through her head all day. She played nearly every pop song she heard perfectly and without hesitation.

17

Her musical horizons had broadened; she now loved R & B as well as pop music, and especially the soft sounds of the Carpenters. "I listened to nothing but Top Forty," she says. "Mainly ballads. I loved Karen Carpenter's voice. I liked easy things for me to pick out on the guitar and sing along with."

Upon graduation from elementary school, Gloria was enrolled in Lourdes Academy, a girls' Catholic high school located on Eighty-fourth Street in Miami. The first year was not easy because she didn't know many of the students. Most of her friends went to the public high school, but her mother had insisted that Gloria attend a parochial school. The summer before entering Lourdes, Gloria had gained too much weight for her five-feet-two-inch frame and was self-conscious about her physical appearance. She seemed to project a sadness to the world outside, and the nuns who were her teachers were concerned.

"I was carrying the burden of the whole world on my shoulders," she acknowledges, "and I think it showed in the way I looked."

At one point, the nuns at Lourdes thought Gloria would also enter the convent after graduation. To this day, she can't figure out why they had that idea. "I don't see myself as a nun. I never did," she says, laughing.

Trying to coax her out of her shyness, the nuns encouraged Gloria to get involved in school activities. She finally got up enough nerve to join the class assemblies, deciding there was no reason why she shouldn't be up on stage performing like so many of the other girls.

Nervously, she'd stand onstage in front of an auditorium filled with her classmates and sing, while strumming her guitar. Gloria had always had a wonderful singing voice. Yet, except for the time when she was a child serenading the women in the old apartment complex, she had never had the opportunity to sing in a public place.

The applause she received from her fellow students when she finished a song encouraged her to continue performing. She enrolled in the one music class the school offered and made new friends. Things were looking up in Gloria's life. But for every positive moment, there would be disappointment around the corner, waiting to strike.

When Gloria turned sixteen, her father went into a VA hospital. The time had come when it was impossible for Gloria and her mother to continue caring for him. He required the care of a hospital, with doctors and nurses nearby. The family's responsibility of constantly watching over him was lifted, but it was harrowing for Gloria to say good-bye. Once, she had wished to be a regular kid and do what others did. Now her wish had come true. But after five years of having her father in the next room, Gloria felt an immense loss at his absence.

To get away from the pain of missing him, she focused all her energy on music and schoolwork. Most of Gloria's time was devoted to her studies, for she planned to attend college and become a psychologist.

She thought of music as her hobby and shared her love of singing with her cousin Merci. Together they would harmonize after school and on weekends. They also began to sing at family parties. By performing, Gloria slowly started to gain the self-confidence she lacked.

Music would help her overcome her shyness, but it wouldn't help her break completely out of her shell. That would only come with time, and encouragement and love from a man who would change Gloria's entire life. His name was Emilio Estefan, Jr.

 **3**

Emilio

The drive for success was strong in Emilio Estefan, Jr.'s family. It's a trait he inherited. Success always meant everything to him, probably because of the loss he witnessed growing up.

The son of Lebanese immigrants, Emilio's father ran an underwear factory in Santiago de Cuba while his mother stayed home to take care of the house and her two sons. Emilio recalls with a laugh that his father was always a strong, business-minded man, "but aside from that he has been a poker player all his life."

For the first thirteen years of his life, Emilio stayed close to home, living in Cuba and trying to ignore what was going on there. His family did not flee to Miami with the others in the late 1950s and very early 1960s. Perhaps because of the business his father had built up, they tried to wait things out. But, unfortunately, the day came when they too would have to leave their lives behind and start fresh in the United States.

"The Communists took everything," says Emilio. "We fled to freedom." He also fled the Cuban draft. In 1966, the thirteen-year-old Emilio and his father went to Madrid to wait for U.S. visas. He was fifteen when he received a student visa and emigrated to Miami.

The palm-tree-lined streets of Miami Beach weren't visible in the part of town where Emilio settled. With no money in his pocket and a limited knowledge of English, he moved into the small apartment where his fifteen aunts and cousins lived. But he wouldn't be there for long.

Emilio possessed a fierce determination to claim his piece of the American dream. He never wavered from the thought that he could make a success of himself in the United States. He figured that with a little hard work, anything was possible. And he was right.

His first concern was to make money so he could bring the rest of his family over. So many people from Cuba were chasing after the same thing, deserting their country and the revolution for a better life. Emilio comments today, "We never left to be rich. We left to live in a free country that believed in free enterprise. And most of the people who left Cuba came to the United States to wash dishes, wash cars. I don't think you're ever going to hear immigrants like the Cuban people complain about Miami or the United States."

Even though he was poorer than he had ever been, Emilio knew he had done the right thing to cross the water and come to this new country. He was grateful for the opportunities the States gave him. Everything he pursued, he accomplished. Gloria says of him, "Wherever there was a business opportunity, Emilio was there."

His ultimate goal was to find something to do that would bring him happiness and financial security. What he was searching for would eventually surface, but first he had to get by from day to day. He found work as a mail boy at Bacardi, the Puerto Rican rum company that had offices and a plant in Miami. And he kept up with his education, graduating from high school and later earning a degree from Miami Dade College.

Along the way, Emilio did whatever he

could in his spare time to make a little extra money. When he bought his first car, a banged-up Volkswagen, he used it to offer to drive Cuban women to the supermarket. He also tried a T-shirt business that failed, and later took ribbons from funeral wreaths and made them into fancy ribbon sashes for beauty contestants. Emilio wasn't going to let anything stand in the way of reaching his goals. He worked for hours, conjuring up new ideas for businesses that would never see the light of day.

While still attending school, Emilio decided to go back to Bacardi, where he began slowly working his way up the corporate ladder. Over the next twelve years he was promoted several times, finally assuming the title of director of Hispanic marketing, a job he wouldn't give up until Miami Sound Machine hit it big.

Music was just a hobby to Emilio at first. He didn't think of it as a career until long after his family was settled in a nice house with a garage where he could practice with other boys in the town. But he did dream of going out and playing in every available club he could find.

As a young boy viewing his first Grammy awards he had wonderful dreams. "I remember thinking, one day I might be in the show," he says. "Just in the show. I never even dreamed that I would be nominated for a Grammy."

Without ever really knowing if his dreams would come true, Emilio walked into a music store one day and bought a used accordion. He began practicing the instrument with a vengeance, playing all his favorite songs by ear. When he thought he was good enough, he made the rounds of the local restaurants. "I walked into an Italian restaurant on Biscayne Boulevard and said to the owner, 'You let me play here, I'll play for free, just for tips,'" he says.

It was an offer the owner couldn't refuse. He set Emilio and his accordion up in the corner of the restaurant and allowed him to pound on it for four hours. Emilio wasn't great, but the customers seemed to enjoy his versions of Cuban rumbas, Italian songs, and polkas. After that night, Emilio realized he had found a new profession. He informed his parents that he wanted to try a career in music.

"Everybody told me I was crazy," he recalls. "My parents told me that music wasn't the right thing to do; it wasn't very secure. But I said that's what I like and that's what I want to do. My brother's an engineer, and everybody else has a career, but they eventually came around and were supportive of me."

The moment he decided to give music his full attention, the opportunities began to pick up for Emilio. His boss at Bacardi had heard of his playing the accordion in the local Italian restaurant, and he called Emilio into his office to ask if he would be interested in playing for a private party.

Emilio excitedly accepted and set out to form his own band. For that first party, he played accordion and added a drummer and conga player for the beat that would keep the party guests dancing. The self-assured budding musician and his band of two played Cuban music for nine hours and left an indelible impression on everyone at the party. It was the first gig of many for Emilio Estefan.

His next step was to put together a real band of young musicians. He added three trumpet players, drummer Enrique "Kiki" Garcia, and bass player Juan Marcos Avila. Dubbing themselves the Miami Latin Boys, they set out to play the Latin sound. Emilio, being the oldest in the band, didn't pay too much attention to the popular music making *Billboard*'s Hot One Hundred charts. The gimmick he wanted for the group was to have them perform strictly Cuban music.

But the others who joined the band weren't that familiar with the Latin rhythms and ballads. They all shared the same background: they were Cuban kids raised in Miami who listened to nothing but American pop music. In those years, the Bee Gees and K.C. and the Sunshine Band were Miami's popular musicians—they played the Miami sound. No one in the younger set dared to play or listen to the music of their parents' generation.

Kiki Garcia, who was five years younger than Emilio and still in high school when he joined the band, says, "I was heavy into disco. I had to buy a bunch of Tito Puente and Celia Cruz records so I could learn the stuff we played at parties."

The then all-instrumental Miami Latin Boys built up a good reputation as entertainers and were hired to play for numerous local get-togethers and weddings. Every weekend, they would pack up their instruments and perform for various functions in town. Somehow, word about this party band spread, even though they weren't the most talented or innovative group in the area.

Carlos Oliva, a Miami bandleader who took on the responsibility of managing the Latin

Boys in the mid-seventies, doesn't brag about their talent. "They were a soft, mellow group to begin with—and not very exciting to watch," he admits honestly. The band was a few years away from playing the sound that would lead them to international success.

As the Miami Latin Boys were carving a niche for themselves in music, Gloria, a senior at Lourdes, was wrapping up her high school education, planning to attend college on a partial scholarship she had earned, and discovering Latin music for the first time in her life.

One day, a young guest visited her music class to give the girls some pointers. That guest was Emilio Estefan, and his eye immediately focused on Gloria, who hung on every word he said. Neither of them realized at the time that they would soon join forces and create one of the most popular Miami bands in history. After addressing the class, Emilio left without even talking to Gloria.

In June 1975, Gloria graduated from Lourdes at the top of her class. That fall, she attended the University of Miami, where she majored in psychology and minored in communications. Gloria later changed her mind, and decided she wanted to be a translator.

She then took those classes that would prepare her for her chosen career.

Over the summer, just for fun, she joined a band that played a lot of Latin music. "I discovered I had Latin music in my blood," she says. "I started as a percussionist with them and did Celia Cruz songs."

Cruz, who is today in her seventies, has been singing salsa for over forty years. With more than seventy albums to her credit, she still packs in crowds whenever she gives a concert. In the 1950s, she was one of Cuba's biggest stars, performing songs like "Canto a la Habana" (Song to Havana) in fancy nightclubs. She is still singing the same songs, but for the younger Cuban generation like Gloria who don't remember Cuba although they are interested in learning the music of their roots.

Known as the reigning Reina de la Salsa, Cruz would become one of Gloria's favorites. "Celia is the queen of salsa," she says. "Ever since I got involved in Latin music, she was the one I would listen to, because she's simply the best there is. Celia's an incredible woman and still a great, energetic performer. She really proves that music can keep you young."

The Latin sound opened new doors for Gloria. The energetic salsa rhythms, which inspire couples to dance the twists and curves of the mambo or the rumba, would become a very important part of her life. Even though she never turned her back on popular music (she says Karen Carpenter and Barbra Streisand were her other musical inspirations), Gloria became completely absorbed in learning the origins of Cuban songs, which her grandmother and mother, who both loved to sing, taught her.

She learned that the Latin sound has its origins in the eighteenth century, when African slaves were brought to work Cuba's sugar plantations. Piano and guitar were mixed with congas and timbales and topped off with big brass. Later, salsa was born, the pulsating sound that was played primarily for dancing. A good salsa song can sometimes run for half an hour, and on that subject, Gloria explains, "We Cubans dance at the drop of a hat."

The perfect place for this music to be played is at a Cuban wedding. It was at such a wedding that Gloria's music career would begin. "My mother dragged me to a wedding where Emilio and the Latin Boys were playing," she recalls. In Little Havana, everyone got to know each other; Gloria and Emilio weren't complete strangers. Their paths had first crossed at her music class where he came to speak; then, only a few months before the wedding, the Latin Boys had played at a party given by her mother. However, Gloria had never paid close attention to Emilio before.

This changed at the wedding, where she couldn't help but watch Emilio as he led the band. His rendition of "The Hustle" on accordion was the number that really impressed Gloria. "I thought, 'This guy is really ballsy,'" she says.

On the outside, Emilio seemed to be having the time of his life; inside, however, he felt different. Though the Latin Boys continued to play gigs all over town, the group hadn't evolved the way Emilio hoped. They were nothing more than the small party band he originally formed. Though they rehearsed and performed industriously, Emilio knew something was missing. He felt the band lacked excitement because they had no lead singer.

Gloria remembers the Latin Boys as "playing only music. Once in a while, they would all take turns singing or they would sing together."

Emilio envisioned bigger things for the group and told this to the band's manager, Carlos Oliva. Emilio, the marketing genius who was earning a good annual salary at Bacardi, was ready to expand the Latin Boys and their sound.

At the wedding, someone passed around the word that Gloria could sing and Emilio asked her if she would join the band for a song or two. Reluctantly, she agreed, stepping up on the band's platform and singing a few standards. With no formal vocal training, Gloria followed her intuition and delivered the songs in her own way. "Of course, the people at the wedding gave me a standing ovation," she says with a laugh, though she didn't think she was *that* good.

Emilio, however, did. He was genuinely impressed with Gloria's singing. "I thought, 'She has such a warm voice, and she's so sincere when she sings,' " he says. As Emilio watched Gloria step off the platform to rejoin her family, he knew she was exactly what he was looking for to add some spice to the Latin Boys.

Now all he had to do was get Gloria to join the band on a regular basis.

 4

Miami Sound Machine

The time was early fall, 1975, when Gloria arrived at Emilio's aunt's house with her cousin Merci. Both girls had been invited to sing with the band, unaware of the fact that Emilio had called Carlos Oliva to listen to them.

Remembering that night, Oliva says, "Emilio told me I better come over to rehearsal. He said there was this girl he had met at a wedding, and she was coming by to audition with her cousin. The girls just wanted to sing, and they didn't want any money. I got there late, and there in the middle of all these neighbors were Gloria and her cousin Merci, harmonizing. It was beautiful."

The girls' soft, melodic voices sparked a thought in Emilio's mind. He wanted Gloria to join the Latin Boys, but hadn't bargained on Merci. If he signed *both* of them, he would have the first Latin band in the area with female lead singers. He made up his mind not to let them leave without trying to convince them to sing with the group on a permanent basis.

When he approached them with his idea, Gloria said no without hesitation. She had just started her freshman year in college and she wasn't going to gamble her future on a band that might never hit the big time. "I didn't even want to think about it," she says today.

But Emilio wasn't the type to take no for an answer. He continued calling Gloria, finally explaining to her that she didn't have to give up going to school. She could sing with the band on weekends and during vacations. He told her the band was a part-time job for him, too. He was still working at Bacardi full-time, earning enough money that he could forget trying to break into music.

Gloria was tempted by Emilio's offer, but she didn't know if it would be the right thing to do. It was only after she received her grandmother's encouragement that Gloria decided not to pass up the opportunity.

"I joined because I loved music, not because

I wanted to perform," she explains. "I didn't want to be in the spotlight, didn't desire it."

In time, all that would change. From the first day Gloria and Merci began singing with the group, things were never the same. It was the end of the Latin Boys and the beginning of a whole new band. Naturally, the name had to be changed, and Miami Sound Machine was chosen. But Gloria, to this day, expresses how much she hated the band's new name.

"We weren't a 'machine,' she says. "The name was very alien to me and didn't have any heart. It was very cold-sounding, but was chosen because it was the disco era and bands had names like that."

For the next four years, Gloria worked at a frenetic pace to keep her grades up in college *and* perform to the best of her ability with the group on weekends. As if all that weren't enough, she also taught guitar in a local community school. She was out meeting and working with people, and the experience helped her a great deal. Though she was still somewhat self-conscious, she wasn't as shy as she had been.

Although she didn't appear ready to stand on stage and sing solo, Gloria wanted to give it a try. After a few shows of singing duets with Merci, and blending in with the rest of the band, Gloria performed her first solo, "What a Difference a Day Makes."

It was a moment of complete triumph for her; from that day forward she would sing a few solo tunes at every show. She had not yet found a distinctive vocal style; that would come in time. When she began singing, she copied the singers she admired. From there, she would develop her own style by performing and, later, writing songs.

Gloria has Emilio to thank for his constant encouragement. He pushed her into the spotlight, convincing her that that was where she belonged. "He saw something in me that I didn't let other people see," she explains, "and he wanted that to come out." Emilio had complete faith in Gloria. There was something about her he didn't know how to describe, but he knew he would be able to bring it to the surface.

At eighteen, Gloria did not feel comfortable with her appearance. While her sister, Becky, comments, "She was ugly!", Emilio describes Gloria as overweight, with very short hair. "But she was beautiful, I mean, even then she was a beautiful girl and you could see it in the skin and the eyes and everything."

After joining the band, Gloria knew it was

time to shed her baby fat. She went on a diet and began the long, slow process of losing first twenty pounds, then twenty more. But the weight didn't come off easily and it was a difficult battle for Gloria. It took her years before she started seeing the results she wanted. Time and again she went off the diet, upset that she wasn't reaching her goal. Because she was working so hard, her energies were depleted and it took strong willpower to avoid a candy bar for a quick pick-me-up. But she stuck it out, trying to eat very little. She knew it would be worth it because she was concerned with looking good while she was singing.

Gloria was beginning to look forward to the band's weekend gigs at weddings, bar mitzvahs, and *quinces* (a Latin coming-out party for fifteen-year-old girls). She was full of enthusiasm, and considered performing "a chance to go to parties and make a little money at the same time. I was really excited. I started thinking, 'Hey, maybe this could be fun.'"

From the beginning, with Emilio's support, Gloria was completely involved with the band. During rehearsals, she had some say as to what they would and would not perform. The Latin Boys were primarily known for playing only Latin music, though they did throw in a pop song every now and then. When Emilio signed Gloria and Merci to sing with the band, it was understood they would experiment with their sound and try different things.

At first, they weren't sure what they wanted to do, but Gloria and Kiki wanted to try more current pop hits. They wanted the band to have a varied sound—a little salsa, a few ballads, and some danceable music. Gloria thought it would be a great change for them; it would ultimately separate them from the other groups in town.

Playing a mix of up-tempo Latin music and Top Forty tunes seemed risky at first. But the band was anxious to diversify. It was very clear that they would not be associated with one particular sound; their tastes were too unformed. Gloria points out, "Salsa is not so ingrained in me that I can't do a legitimate pop tune or vice versa."

The Sound Machine began slowly to move into the top spot as one of the hottest bands in Miami. They soon controlled the party scene, playing the same types of gigs that brought the Latin Boys recognition. The secret of their incredible success was very simple: they played the music people wanted to hear.

As Juan Marcos Avila explains, "Our sound evolved from trying to please all the people. Here in Miami, we have Cubans, Anglos, blacks, South Americans. You have to be very versatile."

It didn't take long before the group was Miami's most successful band. "We'd play Latin music, and then we'd play ballads and pop music," says Gloria. "That helped us to make a good living because people would hire us instead of two bands. In the very beginning, we weren't Anglos playing Latin music or Latins playing Anglo music. We were both, and we satisfied both groups."

Without realizing it, they were playing the beginnings of music that would later be dubbed "the Miami Sound Machine formula." "We had a drummer who could play both salsa and rock beats, and we had a lot of percussion that rock bands didn't know about at the time," explains Gloria. "We'd play a legit salsa tune by Celia Cruz, then play a Top Forty hit next, only we'd add some percussion that wasn't on the original. Since we grew up with both kinds of music, we really didn't have to force things."

By the early part of 1976, Gloria was living in two completely different worlds. Her days were spent in the classrooms at the University of Miami, studying psychology and communications, learning French, and taking classes in music, English, and history. The college, located on 260 acres in suburban Coral Gables, has the distinct honor of being one of the largest independent institutions in the southeastern United States. Here, Gloria maintained a straight-A average, working sometimes around the clock on homework and preparing herself for tests.

After school, she joined Miami Sound Machine for rehearsals. It was a time to get to know the other members better and learn about band life. They all had much in common and were close to the same age, except for Emilio, who was five years older than the rest. Together, this tight-knit clan produced one good, hummable, danceable show.

Gloria has fond memories of those days. "We all got along great, because basically we grew up together," she says. "We all had very similar tastes. And we were striving for one thing—to be successful at what we were doing."

The first few months she performed with the band proved to be an eye-opener for Gloria, a harbinger of things to come. They had played all the weddings and bar mitzvahs they cared to; now it was time to move on.

There are many good bands that really want to break out but are afraid to try because it seems impossible. Others don't even get the chance. Emilio, as leader of Miami Sound Machine, wasn't going to let opportunity pass by. He knew they could accomplish more but they needed time to work on polishing their sound.

There was talk of breaking into the recording business. Kiki and Gloria spent their spare time scribbling down ideas for their own songs. There were no set ideas, no fixed sound. They didn't know how to write songs; after all, they were just teenagers learning together.

After they got the melodies down, the lyrics would begin to flow. Sometimes the songs seemed to write themselves. But the finished product was still rough. They needed someone who could take their music and arrange it.

Emilio asked Raul Murciano, saxman and keyboardist, to expand his talents and arrange the band's original music. Murciano, who had only been part of the Sound Machine a short time, struck up a close friendship with Emilio. Emilio saw raw talent in

Murciano and allowed him the room to spread his creative wings.

Almost immediately, Murciano became romantically involved with Gloria's cousin Merci. The two would begin a hot and heavy romance that ended happily when they tied the knot in 1981. Merci was loyal to the band even though she didn't command as much attention as Gloria did. She mainly sang back-up and performed an occasional duet with her more popular cousin.

The slick sound the band would bring into the mainstream five years down the road was not the sound they ground out that first year. But it was a start, a good, promising start, and it brought the band members even closer together.

There were very few disagreements among them at that time. They all talked excitedly about the next gig, and what the future would hold. Gloria shared the same interest with Kiki—songwriting. And Emilio, who held the band together and acted as its leader, was determined to break into the recording business.

In just one year, this group of young musicians had already grown. Like so many other hopefuls, they wanted to be a commercial band that sold records and made a lot of money. But they didn't make the mistake of not performing any gig they could get. Exposure was the most important thing. They were already successful in Miami; now they wanted to enjoy that same kind of success all over the United States—and the world!

They listened to the sound that was selling and were convinced they captured the formula perfectly. But they would have to wait and see whether or not anyone was going to be interested in signing them to a record deal. For now, it was back to rehearsals and weekend parties.

Gloria looks back on this time as an exciting one! Out front, onstage, she continued developing her talent as the band's featured singer. Offstage, something else was slowly beginning to develop.

Gloria was finding Emilio very attractive, but she didn't know how he felt about her.

As each day passed, Gloria and Emilio discovered each other. He could talk incessantly and she was always ready to listen.

She was shy and polite; he was vibrant and possessed a "naughty" sense of humor that could make Gloria blush. They were encouraging and complimentary about each other's artistic efforts. The truth is, they liked each other instantly, but didn't want to rush into anything they might both be sorry for. According to Gloria, "We didn't want to jeopardize our professional relationship."

They began to spend an increasing amount of time together. But it was always during rehearsals and before shows. They were still "just friends" who spoke of their hopes for their professional futures and traded stories about their childhoods.

Emilio knew of the tragedy in Gloria's life, of her struggle as a child to take care of her father and younger sister while her mother was out working. And his feelings were to protect her, not to let anything else hurt her. He was at a crossroads in his life; he wanted to ask Gloria out, but there were many things standing in his way.

"I liked her," he says, "but I wanted to be sure. Love is something that grows. I remember I told my mother, 'I am not going to make a move on this girl unless I am serious.' I thought, 'If she's in love with me and I'm not ready, she will be destroyed.' I felt she had already been through too much."

On the surface, Gloria and Emilio seemed worlds apart. Gloria was young and inexperienced when it came to love. She had not yet gone on a date with *anyone*.

Emilio, on the other hand, was known as a

ladies' man. He was smooth, cool, and interested in women much older than Gloria. Her younger sister, Rebecca (known as Becky), describes Emilio as "the catch of the town. Handsome, driving around town in his Corvette, he had rubbed so much leather cleaner into those seats that you'd slide forward every time he hit the brakes!" No one would have banked on the two of them getting together.

It was far from love at first sight. Gloria honestly says, "I didn't think he'd be interested in me at all. I had no experience. He had a reputation as a womanizer, which turned out not to be true. And he went out with older women. He would always flirt with me, but he flirts with *everybody*—old men, old ladies. That's just his personality."

All through Gloria's first year with the band, they refrained from mixing business with pleasure. They seemed inseparable at the band's rehearsals and shows, but later, when it was time to go home, they both went their separate ways.

Their relationship remained purely professional, until, unable to deny his feelings any longer, Emilio decided to ask Gloria out for their very first date. It was exactly eight months after she joined the band.

 **5**

Turning Point

The love story of Gloria and Emilio Estefan began at Miami Sound Machine's Bicentennial concert on July 4, 1976. Between sets, he backed her into a quiet corner and told her it was his birthday (she found out later it really wasn't). Then he asked her if she'd give him a little kiss. She did and they went on their first date that same night. Emilio was Gloria's first boyfriend.

Over the next two years, their relationship intensified. It was clear that Emilio cared a great deal for Gloria, but there were times he just wouldn't stop telling her how she could improve herself. She was desperately trying to lose weight and get herself into shape on her own and she didn't need any speeches from him. Unfortunately, though, that didn't stop him.

"He was trying to make me confident," says Gloria, "but I could've smacked him. At the beginning, everybody would always accuse me of being stuck up 'cause I was shy. But a performer can't afford to be shy."

Emilio wanted her to overcome her shyness completely. But the way he went about it upset Gloria *and* her sister Becky, who remembers, "He'd always be saying to Gloria, 'I think you can improve yourself ninety-five percent.' All the time, *'noventa y cinco por ciento.'* God, it drove me crazy. I don't know how she married him."

At times, Gloria remembers having very mixed feelings about him. "It really pissed me off," she asserts. "It really got me so angry that he would do that. I used to say, 'If you think I could improve myself ninety-five percent, then why are you bothering with me now? You only like five percent of me? What if I don't improve? What if I don't change? What if I stay like this?' But Emilio just meant I could come out of myself more."

Her anger prompted her to work even harder on her appearance. During the two years she dated Emilio, Gloria began to emerge as a whole new person. She gained in self-confidence and dropped a substantial amount of weight.

"I used to kid him after that: 'Okay, what am I down to? Seventy-five percent? Sixty?' " She laughs.

Gloria and Emilio didn't try to hide their feelings for each other from anyone. Though Gloria's mother approved of Emilio, she wondered if her daughter should commit herself to the first man she had ever dated. It was a question other family members also had. And there were other doubts. Did those two really know what they were doing? For example, there was a gap of five years between them. Both Gloria and Emilio were convinced that the age difference would not present any serious problems, and they later convinced their families.

As they grew closer personally, the band was beginning to score professionally. In the fall of 1976, Miami Sound Machine recorded its first album entitled *Renacer,* for a small local label. The album had English songs on one side and Spanish on the other. It was produced on a budget of two thousand dollars and all the tunes were original, with some disco pop written by Kiki and ballads composed by Gloria. Latin Americans loved the album and the band's unique blend of disco, ballads, pop, and salsa. Gloria's intoxicating, rich singing style was already creeping through.

Riding on the semisuccess of the album, the group recorded one more for the same label before Emilio decided to invest his own money in recording. Over the next year, two more mostly Spanish-language albums were released on their own label. They sold well.

At first, Miami Sound Machine was simply a regional success. They won legions of local worshipers and it kept some money flowing in. Each band member received a small but steady income and had the thrill of playing to concert audiences.

Miami Sound Machine began performing at stadiums and bull rings in Latin America, drawing sizable crowds. At these shows, the band played all their original songs, something they couldn't do at the local Miami gigs. Says Gloria, "People don't want to dance to something they don't know."

But in Latin America, the band's original sound was creating somewhat of a sensation. They were in demand, and it was a crazy time for them. They went from playing big stadiums one weekend to performing at weddings in Miami the next.

"Finally," says Gloria, "we just decided to

stop playing the Miami parties and concentrate on doing our original music." International superstardom was a long way off, but there was no denying the fact that they were on their way.

For Gloria and Emilio, this newfound success wasn't their ticket to complete security just yet. He continued working his way up in Bacardi's marketing division and she started working part-time as a customs interpreter at Miami International Airport. This gave her the chance to speak Spanish and the two languages she had learned in school—English and French. It was also the training ground for a job as an interpreter, which she was hoping to make a career out of after graduating from college.

But after she graduated from the University of Miami with a degree in psychology and communications, Gloria had a change of heart. She gave up her part-time job at the airport, and decided that music, her hobby, would be her career. The shy student had grown up and would now be lead singer of Miami Sound Machine. Her old world was gone; a new one was opening up before her.

The best Valentine's Day present Gloria ever received was "the engagement ring Emilio gave me," she says. "But he was so impatient, he gave it to me on February twelfth in front of his mother, which I could've killed him for, because how do you react to something like that in front of someone's mother, for God's sake? I was so embarrassed, I didn't know what to do. Emilio's mother, who I get along with very well, was the one who wanted to be there to see my face. I guess he also needed the moral support. Maybe he figured, 'Well, if my mom is there, she won't say no.' "

Seven months later, on her twenty-first birthday, September 1, 1978, Gloria and Emilio were married in a small ceremony. The leaders of Miami's hottest wedding band decided *not* to have a band play at *their* wedding.

"We'd saved some money," says Gloria, "but we decided to spend it on a trip to Japan instead of a reception. Emilio said we should take the time now to go on vacation together, because we may never have the chance to get away again. And you know what? He was right."

When the newlyweds returned home after their honeymoon, it was back to business. With his new bride by his side, Emilio laid down a very careful plan for himself and Gloria. He had three goals for the years ahead and he would work hard to insure he achieved every one. He wanted to start a family with Gloria; he hoped Miami Sound Machine would someday reach the top of the charts; and he dreamed of becoming a record producer.

Emilio knew he was only an adequate musician, and he really didn't plan on just playing with the band forever. But he wouldn't leave performing without knowing he could make a success at producing.

The year 1980 proved to be a milestone for Gloria and Emilio Estefan. Their son Nayib was born, and Emilio decided that Miami Sound Machine would now be a full-time band. CBS International, the Hispanic division of CBS Records located in Miami, signed the band to record four Spanish albums.

It was the first step in the right direction for Miami Sound Machine. Emilio, who was now earning $100,000 a year heading the Hispanic marketing division of Bacardi, quit his job to devote all of his energy to the band.

Things were beginning to fall into place for Gloria. The only event that would cloud her happiness in 1980 was the death of her father. After twelve years of battling multiple sclerosis, Gloria's father was dying. In the last weeks of his life, she rushed to his bedside to be with him and hold his frail hand, as she had years ago. Gloria kept recalling her handsome father's sense of humor, the good times they had shared, how he had risked his life to fight for freedom, and the years she cared for him when he returned home from the war.

Saying a final good-bye to her father was hard. Even though she had known his death was inevitable, she was devastated when it happened. It didn't hit her fully until weeks after the funeral. Throughout the service, she remained calm, clearly in control of both herself and the proceedings. Instead of asking for comfort, she offered it.

She remained strong for her mother and sister and was, as always, the one whom everyone else depended on for sustenance.

When, weeks later, her father's passing became real to her, she refused to let Emilio see the pain she was feeling.

She felt disoriented, and she seems to have dealt with this by trying to blot out the past and start again from scratch.

There was so much to look forward to now that they were going to record for CBS International. Gloria felt a new sense of belonging with the members of Miami Sound Machine; there was such a strong spirit of camaraderie among them. She saw how important music was to them, how disciplined they were. When she married Emilio, who felt the same way about music, Gloria knew that she would now take performing more seriously than ever before. She made up her mind to spend the next few years completely dedicated to her career.

Success was right around the corner for Gloria. In the next five years, she would be thrust into the spotlight and she had to be ready for it. It wouldn't be long before Gloria Estefan's name would be known in all parts of the world. It was going to be a long, uphill climb to the top, but Gloria and Miami Sound Machine were destined to achieve the fame they deserved.

 **6**

A Crossover Dream

From 1981 to 1983, Miami Sound Machine was a household name in Latin America. In Venezuela, Peru, Honduras, and Panama, their albums and singles all shot to number one. They were the first band to come along that was able to play American pop in Spanish. Signed exclusively to the Discos CBS label, Miami Sound Machine recorded *all* their songs in Spanish.

"They [CBS] thought we would sell better in Latin America if we sang only in Spanish," says Gloria, "but we kept the right to record in English because eventually we wanted to try again for the States. But first we decided to concentrate on the Latin American end because it was becoming very successful."

Their music was contagious: sentimental ballads written by Gloria, catchy pop and disco with an ever-so-appealing twinge of samba and salsa. Their success was monumental. Other countries—Brazil, Mexico, and Argentina—soon became conscious of the band's unique sound. Fans snatched up their albums and flocked to their concerts. They were also extremely popular in the Hispanic markets in the U.S., the only regions in the United States where their early albums were distributed.

Miami Sound Machine drove their pulsating sound into both the European and Latin American markets in the span of just three years. CBS, which had initially been anxious to see a return on their investment in the group, was pleased with their success.

In 1981, the band embarked on an extensive concert tour, playing to sell-out crowds all over Latin America. While Nayib was home being raised by his grandmothers and aunts, his parents Gloria and Emilio were traveling the globe. It was clearly a learning experience for them both. Gloria concentrated on songwriting and performing, but Emilio was more interested in learning the business end of running a successful band.

As Miami Sound Machine became a

money-making machine, Emilio took complete control of the band. He put himself in charge of everything, from booking their engagements to hiring musicians—and paying them. All the money earned went first to Emilio, then was parceled out to the others. This was an arrangement that did not thrill the band members, but there was really nothing they could do about it. After all, Emilio, as the group's leader, was responsible for business matters.

Bass player Juan Avila calls Emilio "the magic man. We all looked up to him. He had that special something."

But in 1982, Raul Murciano, the band's ace arranger, saxophonist, and keyboardist, decided to question Emilio. He figured his position was pretty important and Emilio would be straightforward with him. Raul had married Gloria's cousin Merci, and he considered himself one of the family.

Raul felt he and his wife, Merci, should've been offered more than they were earning. They were two of the original members of the band, and they worried about the future, now that they were married.

Unfortunately, Emilio's response was not what Murciano had hoped for, and showed another side of Emilio entirely. "If you asked

Emilio questions about money, he got offended," Murciano states. The question he asked turned into an argument that ended in unhappy results.

According to Murciano, Emilio told him, "If you don't like things as they are, you could take a walk."

Steaming with anger, Murciano impulsively quit the band. His wife Merci, upset over his decision, declared her intention to stay.

But one week after the incident, Miami Sound Machine left for Mexico. They didn't take Merci with them, and therefore left her no choice but to quit.

Oddly enough, though he has a lot of pride, Murciano has no regrets about leaving the band early on. He also holds no grudges over the way Emilio handled the situation. As far as he is concerned, it's all water under the bridge. He says about Emilio, "He is the kind of guy who will manipulate you and you'll end up thanking him."

The year Murciano and Merci left the Sound Machine was, in some respects, the actual beginning of the group's megasuccess. Emilio was already in charge of almost everything it took to keep the band pumping out music. In 1982, he added another job to his growing list of credits, producing the group's album *Rio.*

Though their lives were about as hectic as they could be, Gloria and Emilio reveled in their success. They had nearly everything: popular albums, sold-out tours all through Latin America, and the confidence of CBS. They were raking in huge sums of money and were being profiled in Spanish magazines, along with the rest of the band members. In fact, Avila met his wife, Cristina Saralegui, in 1982 when she interviewed him for Spanish *Cosmopolitan.*

Still, though, they weren't satisfied. To them, this was only the first step. Even though they were selling more records than any other Latin band at the time and gaining more fans than they ever dreamed of, they had another thought in the back of their minds.

They wanted to try and cross over into the American market, a decision executives warned them against. How could they even think of making it in America? They recorded for a Latin label; they didn't sing in English. They were told they had nothing to show America. The label wasn't willing, at first, to record Miami Sound Machine in English.

Bunny Freidus, senior vice president of creative operations and talent for CBS Records International (CRI), explains how determined Gloria and Emilio were from the start. It was their decision to introduce the band's sound in America, but it had never been done before. Freidus explains that no one signed to a Latin distribution company had ever attempted it before. If it worked, Miami Sound Machine would be the first band ever to successfully cross over onto the American pop charts.

Gloria recalls, "Our success started expanding, and although we were only in the Latin market, and we were doing these big international concerts, we thought it was time to grow and try to reach the English-speaking market."

In the years since rock was born, there had been many success stories involving musicians who wandered onto America's shores and became big stars there. Gloria remembers that the groups who made the biggest impact on her were the British bands who had invaded American charts during the 1960s.

When Miami Sound Machine decided to bridge the cultural gap and try their hand at America's pop market, they were told Latin stars were a rarity in mainstream music. The two biggest names that may have paved the way for the Sound Machine were Julio Iglesias and Menudo.

"Menudo and Julio helped open doors for us," says Gloria. "But Julio's success did more for us than Menudo's, because they really didn't have a Latin sound on their records. They put out rock albums with Spanish lyrics, and they appealed to teenagers in the Latin community as well as the United States."

Gloria didn't want the music of Miami Sound Machine to be confined to one audience. She and Emilio were aiming to please all groups, just as they had done playing locally in Miami. The crossover success of their friend Julio Iglesias was very inspiring.

Julio's first English-language album shared the top spot on the charts with megastars Bruce Springsteen and Prince. He broke all records in the United States—and in many other countries. His music was universal, drawing everyone together.

Prior to his arrival on the scene, it seemed an impossible goal for Latin artists to achieve U.S. fame. The Latin superstars of the early 1980s like Jose Jose, Raphael, and Camilo Sesto clung to their heritage rather than stray to the United States. Brazilian superstar Roberto Carlos, who sold millions of albums to Latin fans, was one of the few who tried breaking into the American pop market. CBS enthusiastically released his debut English-language album. Unfortunately, it failed; the label just couldn't sell Carlos to the U.S. market.

Gloria and Emilio knew all the horror stories about other singers, but optimistically thought only of the few success stories. They wanted to branch out by singing in English to achieve success in America, but they vowed never to ignore their Latin fans or their Latin roots.

Gloria and Emilio were different from the other musicians. Unlike even Julio (who grew up in Spain) and Menudo (whose members hailed from Puerto Rico), they resided in the United States. The members of Miami Sound Machine were all children when they crossed the waters and settled in Miami. They all spoke perfect English as well as Spanish. They grew up listening to American pop music and performed many of the current pop hits before turning to their own music. They wanted their songs to be played on all U.S. radio stations, not just the few Miami Latin stations that supported them.

"We live in the United States," Gloria was quoted as saying. "This is our home, this is our country, so it's kind of ironic to us that it was the last place we'd become successful."

Miami Sound Machine wouldn't become well known in the States until they scored a big crossover hit. "Even at home in Miami, to the kids, the adolescents, we were still Latin in their eyes until we recorded something in English," declares Gloria. "After we did that we started getting played on stations *they* listened to."

The push to record an English-language album began back in 1983. Emilio, who had proved to CBS he was skilled at overseeing a project from start to finish, convinced the label to give them a shot at recording in English. But CBS was skeptical; they really didn't want to squander the band's success on a hunch.

Unable to convince them, Miami Sound Machine reluctantly went back into the studio to record another Spanish album. But then Kiki Garcia brought in a rhythmic, sprightly tune he had written called "Dr. Beat." Everyone loved the disco song with a Latin beat, but Garcia's English lyrics weren't translating easily into Spanish.

Taking advantage of the moment, Emilio

approached CBS again about allowing the band to record one song in English. He explained the problem, convincing them how much better "Dr. Beat" sounded with American lyrics. After several long meetings, the executives at the label finally agreed. The band would record the song in English and it would be released as the B side of a Spanish single.

As that ballad began climbing the Latin charts, a curious bilingual Miami radio station disc jockey decided to flip over the record and play side B. From the first day it was played, "Dr. Beat" became an instant hit. The song that introduced Miami Sound Machine to the English-speaking world slowly, but surely, raced up the charts. Radio stations all over America and Europe started giving it airplay. The song would become an international smash, charting in the top five in England and all over Europe. In the United States, it was in the top ten on the dance charts.

The success of "Dr. Beat" was proof enough to the people at CBS that Miami Sound Machine appealed to a vast audience. They were never a company to refrain from striking when the iron was hot. The group's next project would be an *entire* album recorded in English.

As the pace suddenly began to quicken and the incredible pressure mounted, Gloria and Emilio wondered what the band's fate would be. Was their success with "Dr. Beat" just a fluke? After three years of achieving foreign fame, would they click with American audiences when an entire album was released? Would the Europeans who loved their first English single continue to support them?

Now came the real test.

 7

Breaking Down Barriers

The release of Miami Sound Machine's first English-language album, *Eyes of Innocence,* wasn't the smash hit they had hoped it would be. None of the songs, except for the opening one, "Dr. Beat," became chart-topping singles. But the album did generate some noteworthy recognition for Miami Sound Machine, and that really mattered to them.

Eyes of Innocence was primarily a labor of love for the band members. Most of the creative work fell to Kiki Garcia, who was the best at coming up with new song ideas and translating a few of the band's Spanish songs into English. He wrote fast and furiously, as quickly as he could get the notes and lyrics out. He had a knack for re-creating the Latin sound and mixing it neatly with American pop and disco.

Garcia wrote five tracks on the *Eyes of Innocence* album: "Dr. Beat," "Prisoner of Love," "I Need a Man," "I Need Your Love," and "Do You Want to Dance." Gloria composed two hauntingly beautiful ballads, "Love Me" and "When Someone Comes into Your Life." Guitarist Wesley B. Wright's song "OK" was chosen, as was "Eyes of Innocence," an exuberant, bouncy number written by Gustavo Lezcano, the band's harmonica player. The band's Spanish hit "A Toda Maquina" was translated into English and retitled "Orange Express."

Produced by Emilio, the album was recorded at New River Studios in Fort Lauderdale and Blank Tapes in New York. The four founding members of Miami Sound Machine —Gloria, Emilio, Avila, and Garcia—all appeared on the album's front cover. It would be the last time a group shot was used to illustrate a Miami Sound Machine album.

Their first English album went on to sell extremely well in Europe, and in fact it was their European success that made Discos CBS's parent label, Epic, sit up and take notice of the group.

Eyes of Innocence had a lot to offer. The

only thing Miami Sound Machine hadn't accomplished yet was cracking the American pop charts the way they wanted to. And no one could really understand what was standing in their way. *Eyes of Innocence* is perhaps the most pop-oriented collection of songs the band ever put out. In one rich track after another, they managed to display melodic strains and a good, solid, potent beat.

The album is filled to the brim with extraordinarily strong material. Besides the smash hit, "Dr. Beat," "Prisoner of Love," "OK," "Eyes of Innocence," and "Orange Express" unquestionably stand out. The two ballads Gloria wrote showed that she was a talented, knowledgeable young singer *and* songwriter. From the start, Gloria emerged as one performer definitely on the right track—with superstardom not far off in her future.

The singing and playing on their first effort as a crossover band proved that Miami Sound Machine was one new group to be reckoned with. The hotter-than-hot sound of "Dr. Beat" had set the American dance charts on fire and Epic immediately announced plans to distribute the band's next album in larger quantities to the American market.

In the meantime, a promotional concert tour was set in motion to get the band some extra exposure. They would be performing some of the tracks from the *Eyes of Innocence* album, along with their Spanish smash hits, "Renacer," "No Sera Facil," and "Dingui-Li-Bangue." At a concert in Holland, Gloria impulsively decided to add the old conga tune, the Cuban dance that traditionally ends every Miami party and is often played in the streets at carnivals.

At first, Emilio rejected the idea, but eventually he changed his mind. Audiences in Latin America loved it, but Gloria wasn't sure how it would go over in a country like Holland. "We knew they didn't understand the Spanish lyrics," she says, "but they didn't understand the American lyrics of 'Dr. Beat,' either." In the end when they played the old standard, audiences in Holland went wild, showering the band with thunderous applause.

Gloria realized the number was receiving the best responses of anything at their shows —even better than the hit "Dr. Beat." She told Emilio they should write a new song based on the old one, with English lyrics.

On tour, on the train traveling from Amsterdam to London, Kiki Garcia started knocking out the lyrics and music for what would become the "new" Conga song. Tapping his feet as he composed, he put the tune's magic rhythm down on paper note by note. By the time they arrived at their destination, Garcia had completed the song. It was *perfecto;* fundamentally true to their Latin roots, with a beat that would have widespread appeal in the mainstream music marketplace.

They called it "Conga," recorded it, and Epic released it as the first single off their second English-language album, *Primitive Love.* "Conga" was a hit—a *big* hit—and it turned the band into overnight stars. After years of fame in Europe and Latin America, Miami Sound Machine was suddenly—and finally—gigantic in its own country.

Yet, while "Conga" turned Miami Sound Machine into the ultimate crossover band, they still had a few obstacles to overcome before they could fully enjoy life at the top of the U.S. charts. One producer rejected their song because he felt it was not easily classified.

"I'll never forget when we first did 'Conga,'" Gloria recollects. "This producer told us that the song was 'too Latin for the Americans, and too American for the Latins.' I said, 'Great, that's exactly what we want. We're a mix.'"

The band also initially had problems with some radio stations that didn't want to play the "ethnic" song at all. "When 'Conga' came out, a lot of Top Forty stations said, 'We'll never play this,' and then it ended up becoming their number-one request," remarks Gloria.

The song "Conga" crossed barriers, struck chords in many hearts, and was bought by all age groups. It was so enormously popular that it even surprised Gloria and Emilio to some extent. It remains definitively one of the great singles of the eighties. Both Gloria and Emilio feel that letting their Latin fans know they wouldn't ignore them had a lot to do with their incredible success. "We snuck in the back door," says Gloria. "But our old audience knew that 'Conga' was more Latin than everything else we'd done and felt that, rather than turning our backs on them, we were bringing something Latin into the Anglo market. So they stood by us and were proud."

Emilio, who echoes Gloria's words, reflects, "I think we succeeded where so many other crossover acts failed because we stayed honest. We put out 'Conga' instead of a rock and roll song."

"Conga" was the first single to simultaneously crack the pop, black, dance, and Latin

*T*he key to our success has been our ability to actually write—not translate—our original music and lyrics," explains Gloria.
(Photo: David Fisher/London Features)

*E*ighteen-year-old Gloria
(*middle right*) had no plans to
sing professionally until Emilio
Estefan (*top*) convinced her to
join his band in 1975. This is
one of the first photos of Miami
Sound Machine's early years.
(*Photo: The Miami Herald*)

*T*he four original
Miami Sound
Machinists were
(*left to right*) Emilio,
Juan Marcos Avila,
Gloria and Kiki
Garcia. Their big
crossover hit "Conga"
turned the band into
overnight stars in the
United States.
(*Photo: Ron Wolfson/
London Features*)

*T*he crowd cheers as
an energetic Gloria
dances to the beat of
Miami Sound
Machine's smash
1987 hit "Rhythm Is
Gonna Get You."
(*Photo: Ron Wolfson/
London Features*)

Gloria and Miami Sound Machine got the 1989 American Music Awards off to an exciting start by opening the show. They were named the year's Best Pop/Rock Group. *(Photo: Celebrity Photo)*

Gloria, surrounded by the members of Miami Sound Machine during their 16-month smash *Let It Loose* concert tour. Kiki Garcia *(on Gloria's left)* would leave the band after their final concert in the Miami Arena. *(Photo: Ron Wolfson/ London Features)*

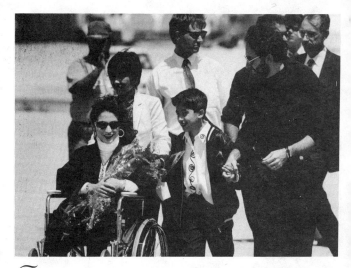

*F*amily, friends and fans gathered at Miami International Airport on April 4, 1990 to welcome Gloria home after her accident and surgery. Having Emilio and Nayib by her side helped her through the ordeal. *(Photo: Brian Smith/The Miami Herald)*

*G*loria at home with her son Nayib. He wants to follow in his mom's musical footsteps and become a singer in the future. *(Photo: Brian Smith/ The Miami Herald)*

*F*rom tight black pants to bangled bolero jackets to this flaming red outfit, vivacious Gloria looks terrific in everything she wears. *(Photo: Scott Downie/Celebrity Photo)*

"*I*'m of the first (Cuban-American) generation that grew up in the United States, and in a way I've had the best of both worlds," says Gloria. *(Photo: Greg DeGuire/Celebrity Photo)*

*W*hat is Gloria and Emilio's secret recipe for their happy marriage? Despite their phenomenal success, they have remained an incredibly down-to-earth, unpretentious couple who still like to do the same things they did when they were dating. *(Photo: Scott Downie/Celebrity Photo)*

Strutting her stuff live onstage, Gloria exclaims, "Performing is one of the best feelings I know!" (Photo: Ron Wolfson/London Features)

Gloria, as she appeared in her video for "Can't Stay Away From You." She describes the filming as very awkward, saying, "It was weird to have to touch another man and make it believable." (Photo: Ron Wolfson/London Features)

"I'm always a little nervous right before I go onstage," admits Gloria, who rules the stage with her salsified pop music. "I try to relax and breathe real slowly about ten times before I go out!" (Photo: Ron Wolfson/London Features)

*G*loria is not only a talented singer/dancer but also a song-writer. Her specialty is heart-wrenching ballads like the Top Ten hits "Words Get in the Way," "Anything For You," and "Don't Wanna Lose You." *(Photo: Ron Wolfson/London Features)*

*J*ulio Iglesias is one of Gloria's closest friends. "He's the ballad king," she praises. "I don't think anyone does a ballad better than him." *(Photo: Scott Downie/Celebrity Photo)*

*M*eeting other celebrities is always fun. Actor Patrick Swayze went to see Gloria's concert at the Greek Theatre and later met the dynamic entertainer at the party in her honor. *(Photo: Scott Downie/Celebrity Photo)*

*G*loria's Miami home is a lavish, but comfortable, Spanish-style hacienda, with a red tile roof and large expanses of glass.

*O*ne of the perks of success—the family car is a Rolls-Royce.

charts. It was such a monster hit that some people believed it would fuel a new Latin dance craze across the country. Like the mambo or the cha-cha of the 1950s, the conga was predicted to be the new dance everyone would be doing in the 1980s. And while the song was sitting pretty on the top of nearly every music chart, this almost came true.

In June 1986, at a concert in Burlington, Vermont, 11,142 people formed the World's Longest Conga Line, dancing to Miami Sound Machine's music. The event was extremely moving. Kiki Garcia was quoted as saying, "We finally have the response from America that we have wanted all these years."

The attempt to turn the conga into the national rage unfortunately never succeeded. It did, however, earn Gloria Estefan and Miami Sound Machine a listing in the 1988 Guinness Book of World Records for participating in the longest conga line in history—119,984 people at the annual Calle Ocho Festival in Miami.

Their second English-language album, *Primitive Love,* was, undoubtedly, the band's big breakthrough. Recorded at New River International Sound Studios and produced by Emilio, it would spawn three Top Ten hit singles, ("Conga," the effervescent "Bad Boy," and Gloria's superb ballad "Words Get in the Way") and sell 2 million copies worldwide. In the U.S. alone, the album sold 1.5 million copies. Some critics were enthusiastic in their reviews of the album, while others accused the band of playing "watered-down salsa."

In response to that criticism, Gloria continuously told reporters, "We could have told them that. We can get up there and do a legit salsa song, but that's not what's within us, it's not where we are. In a sense we *are* 'watered-down salsa.' It comes from being transported to another country."

The group loved the fact that people around the globe were dancing to their music, even though they didn't consciously plan on being cast in the dance-market mold. Gloria, who was always ready to speak out on this subject, said about the band's music, "To be honest, I don't know how to describe our sound. We're very high energy but we also write ballads . . . slow tunes and middle-of-the-road [tunes] that are between dance tracks and ballads. We're not necessarily trying to aim at the dance market. But I have to be honest and say that 'Conga' and 'Dr. Beat' were released as twelve-inch singles to dance clubs, and that's how they became hits. Those records probably never would have been noticed if the dance clubs didn't exist."

Having to explain the reasons for the band's sound was very frustrating at first. Later, Gloria happily discovered that the music spoke for itself. Beginning with *Primitive Love,* Miami Sound Machine's salsified pop music was looked upon as something fresh in a market that was becoming repetitious and increasingly stale.

In her review in *Audio* magazine, Paulette Weiss wrote, "The Miami Sound Machine blew in from southern climes and burned a hot little hole in the radio airwaves with its first major-label single, 'Conga.' The exciting Latin percussion blew away the cooler sounds of British and British-influenced American rock. Pour yourself a tall, cool, iced Passion Punch, put on your sunglasses, and flip on the old air conditioner before you tangle with *Primitive Love.* It's hot, hot, *hot.*"

In her description of Gloria, Weiss said, "Gloria Estefan's solid, sophisticated vocals blaze out on cuts like 'Conga' and 'Primitive Love' and waft out gently on delicate ballads. The hit 'Bad Boy' has been encouraging young men all over the country and beyond to think naughty thoughts about lead singer Estefan, whose good looks only exacerbate the situation."

Gloria's crisp, clear delivery of some songs, especially the fine ballads "Words Get in the Way," "Falling in Love," and "You Made a Fool of Me," reminded many other reviewers of Karen Carpenter.

Of the comparison, Gloria says, "I loved her voice. People compare us a lot, because the timbre of our voices is similar. But she was different. I've loved R & B singing my whole life, and it gives me a little different phrasing sometimes."

Primitive Love marked many firsts for Miami Sound Machine, most notably their association with Joe Galdo, Rafael Vigil, and Lawrence Dermer, known as the Jerks. How did the Jerks get so involved with Miami Sound Machine? As the story goes, Galdo, Vigil, and Dermer were nothing more than struggling musicians when Emilio Estefan met them. At the time, they were working on a commercial jingle and preparing songs for a salsa-aerobics project titled *Salsa-cize*. Emilio, recognizing their talent instantly, hired them first to play backup on the *Eyes of Innocence* album, then to write original songs for the band. *Primitive Love* contains three new tunes that they composed exclusively for Gloria to sing, and four tracks from *Salsa-cize*, including the hit "Bad Boy."

The relationship between the Jerks and Emilio was never completely smooth. They always had their differences of opinion. But somehow they managed to work out the kinks and avoid arguing. The whole creative process of writing and recording music was too important to all of them.

Joe Galdo says that Miami Sound Machine splintered into two groups when *Primitive Love* hit the charts. There was the original band, with members Garcia and Avila, who performed both before audiences and on recordings, and there was the studio band, consisting of Galdo, Vigil, and Dermer and some session musicians, who performed only on the recordings and wrote and arranged all the songs. According to Galdo, the Jerks introduced programs of synthesizer and rhythm that were eventually used at all Sound Machine concerts.

Joe Galdo was proud to be part of the group. And he has always had nothing but good things to say about Gloria, whom he describes as "naturally musical and a real hard worker. No prima-donna groove. If there was something wrong with a track at four in the morning, she'd say, 'Okay, let's work on it.' "

The three songwriters/musicians composed seven of the ten tracks on *Primitive Love*, but Galdo exclaims, "You need a magnifying glass to see our credits. The sound you hear on that album—what people started calling the Miami Sound—that's not the band, that's *us*. All you have to do is check out their old albums to hear the difference."

It's true the Jerks and songwriting partner Suzi Carr contributed greatly to the album. But it's also true that two of the songs they did *not* write became smash-hit singles— "Conga," which was written by Garcia, and "Words Get in the Way," which was written by Gloria. *And* many critics have defined "Conga" as the song that began the now-legendary Miami Sound.

But the important thing was that the band was successful and would become *more* successful. That was reason enough for Galdo, Vigil, and Dermer to stay with Miami Sound Machine for two more years and through one more blockbuster album before calling it quits.

Another first for Miami Sound Machine with *Primitive Love* was Epic Records's insistence on featuring Gloria as the group's star. Though Miami Sound Machine's name was on the album, the cover's art chosen was a close-up portrait of Gloria—*alone.* Photos of the group, Emilio, Garcia, Avila, and Gloria, appear on the album's back cover. The four separate casual snapshots, one of each band member, were shot by Michael Wray at Parrot Jungle in Miami.

David Glew, who is president of Epic Records and in charge of marketing Gloria and Miami Sound Machine domestically, remembers when the band first signed with Epic. The label immediately became interested in promoting Gloria as a separate entity and focused entirely on her image. Glew did not want to limit her. "It was very important that she was not treated as strictly a pop act," he says. "We wanted to broaden her base. Part of the initial plan involved touring to get her out there to Middle America."

But Epic was very careful in manipulating Gloria's image—and the image of Miami Sound Machine. They didn't push them too hard or too fast. They released only a few singles and waited until those bulleted up the charts. When it came time to start the band's American tour, they took it one step at a time. Miami Sound Machine didn't begin by playing the big stadiums in the U.S. Instead, they were booked to play small theaters and fairs before moving up to larger showcases like the

Westbury Music Fair and then Radio City Music Hall in New York.

The more tickets they sold in the United States, the more CBS concentrated on marketing the group to the record-buying public. That first concert tour consisted of some small dates in the Midwest, with the majority of their U.S. leg in the Eastern states. The rest of the time they traveled to the Latin American countries where they were a stadium-level attraction.

Gloria was never one to cancel a concert date, because she never wanted to disappoint her fans. She does admit that playing in some countries proved more nerve-wracking than playing in others. In 1985, Miami Sound Machine burst onto the stage in troubled El Salvador accompanied by three bodyguards with Uzi machine guns. Gloria, who played before forty thousand screaming fans, remembers they were surprised when their audience greeted them with fireworks. "When they went off," says Gloria, "we all hit the deck. The audience just laughed."

The band now consisted of nine members, but most fans and some critics cited three outstanding talents in the group—Gloria, Emilio, and Kiki Garcia.

If Gloria was its voice, and Emilio was its

leader, Kiki was known as the heartbeat of the group. He was quickly becoming a favorite and was dubbed "the spirit of Miami Sound Machine." Onstage, Garcia was constantly in motion. One minute the spotlight was on him as he pounded the drums; the next he'd be up there dancing right alongside Gloria. Garcia could do everything and audiences loved him!

Garcia, Avila, Gloria, and Emilio became known as the "Sound Machinists." They posed playfully for photographers and seemed to get along fabulously—onstage and off!

When *Primitive Love* was released, Kiki was twenty-seven years old and just divorced; Avila was twenty-eight, the father of three and happily married to Cristina Saralegui, who was slowly working her way up to becoming talk-show host of a local Miami TV show. Gloria confirmed the rumors of the band's blissful relationship by saying, "The four of us are very close. We get along fine. When we don't, we talk out our differences in Spanish."

The year that brought Gloria international success was also the year of her tenth high school reunion. But the girls she graduated with didn't recognize Gloria—and neither did the nuns at Lourdes. Gloria had come a long way from the withdrawn schoolgirl who sang nervously at class assemblies.

She now commanded the stage as the lead singer of a band that was packing stadiums, including Miami's Orange Bowl. The last time Gloria had seen the stadium was when she was living in the tiny apartment behind it. She never dreamed that a day would come when she would be playing her music in that stadium, and others like it. When her former teachers at Lourdes saw Gloria flying across the stage, they couldn't believe it.

"They were very surprised," says Gloria, "at the change in me. Not only physically but just the way I had *changed.* I don't think they ever expected me to be out there singing in front of thousands of people."

The success of Miami Sound Machine's *Primitive Love* album not only firmly established the band as undisputed celebrities, but it brought Gloria to the attention of the world as a very talented singer/songwriter. The limelight was securely focused on her as she became the year's hot new superstar.

The band had achieved international stardom and Gloria was proud of the fact that they had successfully introduced the Latin sound into the pop market. In an interview, she explained, "What has really helped us cross over is the fact that a lot of dance music is influenced by percussion and percussion is part of the Latin sound. What happened with 'Conga' is that *conga* is an actual rhythm, an actual Latin dance, and we just had to decide how far we wanted to take it. We finally said, 'If we're going to do it, let's go all out.' We combined the traditional conga with a very steady dance beat. That way we knew it would be a little bit more palatable to the pop audience. We're very happy that we have a new audience that at one time knew nothing about Latin music and now they love it!"

 **8**

Let It Loose

Miami Sound Machine became *more* than just a pop/rock group to the Cuban people of Miami. At home, the success of *Primitive Love* made their neighbors embrace them as *family*. Gloria and Emilio, at the head of the family, became unofficial role models for the city's Cuban population.

While Gloria and Emilio were looked upon as Miami's most positive, level-headed, and successful couple, the city's reputation was suffering at the hands of a new TV show filmed in Miami. The slick but violent cop drama, *Miami Vice,* would become one of the hottest shows on TV, even though many were not pleased with its portrayal of the criminal underworld evolving in the city. The current crime wave had already crippled the former vacation paradise and Miami didn't need any more exposure than it already had.

The show, however, was a huge hit, and it made a star out of Don Johnson. One of its most appealing qualities was the inclusion of contemporary music. It was one of the reasons why America was tuning in every week.

By its second season on the air, the producers had signed a host of big-name music guest stars to appear on the show. Some artists, such as Phil Collins, Glenn Frey, and John Taylor (of Duran Duran), even had roles in the episodes.

Most of music's hottest talent gave their support—and their songs—to *Miami Vice*. But when the producers asked Miami Sound Machine to make a guest appearance, Gloria wanted no part of it. "They wanted us to be onstage performing at a party where a drug bust was going to take place," she says. "We turned it down and they never asked us back. But I didn't want to do that."

Gloria explains that the show hurt the city's reputation. "All the show did was give Miami a glamorous edge. It really didn't help it at all," she says. "I never had a problem living here. Of course, there are problems that we have to do something about, but the press tends to write only about the bad things because good news doesn't sell papers."

The one bit of good news the press *did* write about was the success story of Miami Sound Machine, local band that hit the big time. The ultimate accolade came when Miami's mayor gave the group the key to the city and renamed a Dade County street Miami Sound Machine Boulevard in their honor.

In an interview after the ceremonies, Gloria, who at the time lived on the boulevard, proudly stated, "The city council voted to change it, and our neighbors were happy about it. While *Miami Vice* has conjured up images of drugs and violence, we're goodwill ambassadors for the city."

Nineteen eighty-six had been a very busy and prosperous year for Gloria and the band. Working nonstop, they were asked to record "Hot Summer Nights" for the sound track of the hit Tom Cruise film *Top Gun*. Another original tune, "Suave" (written by Gloria and Kiki), was recorded for the sound track of the movie *Cobra*, which starred Sylvester Stallone.

On their nine-month world tour, the group represented the United States at the Tokyo Music Festival and won a grand prize of

$16,666. They also signed a seven-figure deal to do Pepsi commercials worldwide in both English and Spanish. *Billboard,* the music-industry bible, named them Best New Pop Artists and Top Pop Singles Artists for 1986. With one big smash English-language album to her credit, Gloria Estefan was being hailed as one of the most charismatic performers to hit the music world since Madonna and Michael Jackson.

But all that work was beginning to take its toll on Gloria. The constant traveling, packing and unpacking, catching the right flights and staying on a hectic schedule had some dizzying effects. After months on the road, Gloria needed a rest. She and Emilio missed their son and wanted to spend some time with him. The schedule the band had grown accustomed to came to an abrupt halt. The work continued—only at a slower pace. "We need to stay home a while," Gloria told one reporter. "We need time to write and record."

According to Larry Stessel, product manager for Epic Records, Gloria also needed time to "grow" after *Primitive Love.* While she was taking a much-needed break to compose new songs for the band's next album, Stessel and the executives at CBS were planning a fresh marketing plan, complete with a new advertising campaign that would strengthen Gloria's appeal to consumers. According to Stessel, packaging and marketing an artist is just as important as the music they play.

With Gloria and Emilio, he discussed the new ideas he had for the group. "They needed someone to believe in them," he says. "We talked about changing the name of the band, about image."

What was initially important to Stessel was to promote Gloria in a big way. "She was the one constant in the band. We chose to provide focus by bringing her out. We immediately went out and did a photo session with one of the top photographers in Los Angeles. We started on the clothes."

Wardrobe designers were hired to change Gloria's style, and makeup specialists changed her look. The dark lipstick had to go. Emilio asked Samy, a close friend who had been Gloria's hair and makeup artist since the early days, to add his expertise to her transformation.

"We got into earth tones," says Samy. "Softer. An international look. She's a diamond. Emilio and I wanted to polish her up."

While the music was being written, arranged, and recorded, a whole new image was being created for Gloria. The first thing they did was change the name of the band from Miami Sound Machine to Gloria Estefan and Miami Sound Machine. They wanted people to know *her* name. "I felt there was a lot of marketing confusion—that she needed a change of direction," says Tommy Mottola, president of CBS Records. "We made Gloria look like a star, and focused the group more into the mainstream."

By the time they were finished, Gloria Estefan had gone through one of the most amazing make-overs in pop history. With the release of the group's next album, *Let It Loose* in 1987, she had turned into a musical swan.

But bringing Gloria out front was not the only change at this time. *Let It Loose* would mark the end of an era for veteran "Sound Machinists." Key band members Juan Marcos Avila and Wesley Wright had already left. In their place, Emilio hired young musicians right out of the University of Miami's music department. This decision didn't sit well with Kiki Garcia, who felt that he was being overlooked and shoved into the background when, in reality, he had helped create their sound.

Garcia stayed on through the *Let It Loose* tour and co-wrote two of the band's next biggest hits with Gloria, the snappy "1-2-3" and the now-classic "Rhythm Is Gonna Get You." But he was very unhappy with what had happened to the band he used to know so well, the band he grew up playing with. According to Garcia, the "old" Miami Sound Machine was gone; in its place was "Gloria and Emilio telling a bunch of hired musicians what to do."

At the time, few people outside the tight-knit Miami Sound Machine "family" knew of the troubles affecting the band members. For the most part, nothing was brought out in the press until later—much later. The main thing to Gloria, Emilio, and Epic Records was the release of *Let It Loose*. They saw to it that no negative stories circulated that might affect album sales.

Someone once said, "You're only as good as your last record," and those words echoed in Gloria's mind. She knew the band would have to outdo themselves if they wanted a bigger success than *Primitive Love*. But they were also careful not to be overly ambitious with the new collection of songs. Gloria and Emilio announced they weren't going to stray from their already popular sound; they were just going to enhance it, bring out another side of it.

For example, even though "Rhythm Is

Gonna Get You" has a Latin edge, Gloria says, "It's bembe, a different rhythm than conga. People don't realize that each Latin culture has its own rhythms. It's impossible to educate everyone about everything but we can try and explore these things. At least they'll be introduced to something."

Gloria found herself, once again, with very little free time. As the songwriter on some tracks as well as vocalist, her job consisted of more than merely walking into the studio, singing her part, and walking out. She was completely involved in the whole process of piecing the album together—from idea to finished product.

Basically, the recording of the *Let It Loose* album went smoothly and the group stayed on a good schedule. The biggest problem arose with Gloria's ballad "Anything for You." Emilio recalls, "Recording the music for *Let It Loose* wasn't a difficult task, but it was scary when we did 'Anything for You.' We originally cut the song in one day, but then seventy-two hours before we were going to press the record, Gloria said she was unhappy with her vocal performance. We listened and finally decided that her vocals were great—it was the music that wasn't happening. So, three days before we had to turn in the master tapes, we decided to re-record all the music around Gloria's voice. We felt that Gloria's vocal was so special we weren't going to mess with it, so we re-recorded all the instruments. We didn't sleep for three straight days. Talk about exhaustion!"

The song was the only track on the album that Emilio produced himself. When "Anything for You" was played for the record company, Emilio remembers, "Nobody liked it. Nobody wanted to include it on the album. I said it was a hit and Gloria backed me up. We have been very lucky. They agreed to include it and it was the first number-one single."

Almost instantly, *Let It Loose* was an international smash. It knocked down the competition and made *Billboard*'s chart in a matter of a few weeks. *Let It Loose* stayed on the charts for more than two years and spun off four Top Ten hits: "Anything for You" (number one), "1-2-3" (number three), "Rhythm Is Gonna Get You" (number five), and "Can't Stay Away from You" (number six).

The album also expanded their international superstar status in Latin American countries and shot to the number-one spot in Europe, Australia, and Canada. *Let It Loose* would go on to sell more than four million copies, one million in England alone.

The album was a technical masterpiece. It was recorded at Criteria Studios in Miami and produced by Emilio Estefan and the Jerks, Joe Galdo, Lawrence Dermer, and Rafael Vigil, who wrote and arranged five of the ten tracks. From the opening number, "Betcha Say That," the album was a series of stylishly arranged, peppery Latinesque songs. Guest artists—saxophonist Clarence Clemons, jazz pianist Paquito Hechevarria, and bass player Will Lee—added to this irresistible package of rhythms, sharp percussion, and brassy horns.

Let It Loose has everything: fiery, powerful dance tunes like the title song, "Surrender," and "Rhythm Is Gonna Get You" and the softer, slower ballads "Can't Stay Away from You" and "Anything for You." Galdo, Dermer, and Vigil arranged their song "I Want You So Bad" with terrific synthesized instrumental sounds behind Gloria's vocals.

The critics all raved about Gloria's latest album, even though they weren't completely in favor of her name being placed above the band's.

People magazine called it "a remarkably varied album . . . a fancy concoction of pop, Latin and disco modes . . . slick and tuneful . . . Estefan has a rich, insinuating style."

According to *Stereo Review,* "Gloria Estefan is not just another singing pretty face. She is a formidable vocalist, and she helped write half the songs here along with her cofounders of Miami Sound Machine, Emilio Estefan and Enrique ('Kiki') Garcia."

Paulette Weiss, reviewing the CD in *Audio* magazine, wrote, "Sound snaps out of this compact disc like the crack of a whip. Crisp and sharp, with a bite that leaves its mark, the production on the new Miami Sound Machine CD, *Let It Loose,* is about as good as it gets."

It was clear the band had grown in scope since its first attempt at cracking the U.S. market. And with this, their most electrifying album to date, they were now being fully recognized in all corners of America, not to mention the world.

But with this new kind of success came changes, both good and bad. And Gloria was not completely ready to accept *all* of them.

 **9**

Success and Separations

In 1987, Emilio Estefan officially retired from playing with Miami Sound Machine. He wanted to devote more time to producing, publishing, and managing the band and other musicians. He also wanted to spend more time with Nayib.

"It was a mutual decision for Emilio to stay home with our son," says Gloria. "Nayib starts missing us when we're touring. I would rather he have one parent with him than be totally left alone. Missing both of us would be very traumatic for him. In the past, Emilio brought him on tour with us in the summer. Nayib has been exposed to a lot of experiences that other kids never get."

But it wasn't the kind of life they really

wanted for Nayib. When September rolled around, if the family were not yet home from their summer tour, they would hire a tutor for Nayib and he was taught his schoolwork on the road. However, they were not happy about his getting his education while traveling around the world.

When it came time to begin the scheduled ten-month *Let It Loose* tour, Gloria and Emilio decided to separate for the first time in twelve years. "In the beginning I have to admit it was very tough on me because I was used to being with Emilio all the time," says Gloria. "For nine out of the twelve years we have been together, we spent twenty-four hours a day with each other, so it was difficult to get used to being apart."

On the homefront, Emilio missed Gloria just as much as she missed him, but they made the adjustment for the sake of their young son. "Emilio and I hurt so much when we had to leave Nayib, even though he was always with Emilio's or my family," Gloria confesses. "We felt that once Nayib started school, he needed something more than being tutored on the road with twenty-five men. So we felt less guilty when Emilio decided to stay home with him."

Gloria refers to the time she spent away

from Emilio as "a growth process for both of us. Together, I used to lean on him a lot. Suddenly, I had to be by myself, be on my own, make decisions that normally he would make. It really matures you and lets you grow, so it's been good for us."

As Gloria embarked on the worldwide *Let It Loose* tour, she had no idea it would be so successful. Originally, she told Emilio when she returned after the ten months, she would take time off to have another baby. Then the album started selling in the millions and "Anything for You" hit number one in almost every country. Six additional months were added to the tour and the band began playing in much larger venues.

Gloria's sister, Becky, was her assistant for the tour and remembers, "We went from playing five-thousand-seat halls to playing thirty thousand in two weeks after the release of 'Anything for You.' "

The highly successful sixteen-month *Let It Loose* tour took Gloria and the band from one sold-out performance to another. In the first ten months she played in Japan, Southeast Asia, Canada, and the U.S. An additional six months took the pint-sized superstar all over Europe, where she played shows for her fans in Madrid, Amsterdam, London, Paris, Stockholm, Rome, and Milan.

At the time, conquering Europe was Gloria's main concern. Even though the band had been very popular there, the *Let It Loose* album hadn't been doing well in the U.K. The release of "Anything for You" changed its fate. As the single began climbing the charts, the album *Let It Loose* was removed from stores and eventually re-released with the new title *Anything for You* after the successful song. The packaging was also changed, although the album's contents stayed the same.

All of a sudden Gloria Estefan found herself in demand! While in England, she received invitations to countless parties and openings. In London, she performed at the prestigious Prince's Trust Concert and was amazed by the response she received from the audience. Says Lisa Kramer, director of marketing and sales for CRI, "The album, at that point, just exploded."

The accolades tumbled around Gloria's ears like an avalanche. Everyone involved with the world tour would remember the time spent in London as the high point of the trip. Bunny Freidus refers to the band's success in Europe as one of its greatest victories. "The album sold a million-and-a-half copies in England," she says. "If you compare that to the American market, with a population that is five times larger, it sold the equivalent of seven and a half million here in the States."

To be able to hop from one country to the next and appeal to everyone is extraordinary. Gloria had achieved the impossible. She was one artist who was capable of universally touching everyone with her songs. That's truly the mark of a great performer. There haven't been many who could appeal to a spectrum of audiences simultaneously.

Nineteen eighty-seven would be one of the greatest years of Gloria's career, both publicly and privately. During her sixteen months on the road, she went on a strict and strenuous training program. Her sister explains that Gloria began working out nonstop because she missed Emilio and Nayib. "When she gets depressed, she exercises for hours," says Becky.

By the time she was halfway through the tour, Gloria had shaped her body into its best physical condition. She toned up her thighs, stomach, and waist, losing the extra poundage and replacing it with muscle. She was a completely changed woman; even the structure of her face was different. Her eyes seemed bigger, her nose seemed smaller, and her cheekbones were prominent. In the year that had passed since her first press photos were taken, Gloria seemed to be almost another person. Dressed in a designer black leather jacket, black boots, and skin-tight black leather pants, Gloria Estefan now *looked* like a real American pop/rock star.

Miami Sound Machine was booked to play in nearly every city and country on the map. Whoever wasn't familiar with Gloria Estefan and the band would be by the end of their *Let It Loose* tour. But one country was deliberately left out of the tour, the one Gloria will *never* perform in—Cuba.

"It's a very personal thing," she says. "I'd never play in Cuba while it's a communist country. It would be like slapping my father in the face and I really don't want to do it. There are many places in the world where I still haven't performed that I could be performing without having to do that."

There are too many bad feelings between Fidel Castro's government and Gloria. The band is as popular in Cuba as they are in any other country, but their name has been changed to MSM, to avoid any reference to Miami.

This subject seems to constantly distress Gloria, who explains, "Everyone knows.

'Conga' went to the top of the charts in Cuba. They sell our records on the black market; they make money off us."

Politics is not one of Gloria's favorite subjects. In fact, she tries to avoid discussing politics. "Talking about politics and religion is a surefire way of getting in deep trouble," she says. "And what I say is not going to affect anyone or change anything. My business is not that—my business is to try to evoke emotion."

Gloria says she has always stayed away from politics "because it affected our entire lives, so it's not easy for me to get involved in politics. That's the main reason why I left it out of my music, because the most beautiful thing in my life is music and for me personally to involve politics in that would be like ruining it for me."

Unfortunately, Gloria's roots and her views on Cuba were made public when, in August 1987, she and Miami Sound Machine were invited to perform at the closing ceremonies of the international Pan American Games in Indianapolis. The games were marred by uncontrollable tension between Miami-based exiles and Cuban athletes. Cuba, the second-biggest winner at the games, threatened to boycott the closing ceremonies if the band showed up to play. Cuban delegates called the invitation of Miami Sound Machine a provocation.

Gloria found the whole thing ridiculous. "They were actually worried about this kind of stuff," she says. "It's very funny to me because I am over here making music like 'Bad Boy,' 'Conga,' and 'Words Get in the Way,' and they're over there worried about it. That shows how paranoid that whole system is. It's built on paranoia [that goes] to the extent that they can't allow people to see anything like that for fear of what they'll make of it."

Gloria was determined to perform. She trusted her instincts, which told her nothing really dangerous would happen. Even though the band continued to receive death threats, Gloria didn't let it bother her. Under heavy security, Miami Sound Machine performed on schedule. The Cubans, who wisely chose not to boycott the ceremony, sat quietly. But the band's performance was blacked out in Havana.

"They allowed it to be played on the radio," says Gloria. "But I really think Miami is a thorn in Cuba's side. People who traveled to Cuba brought back newspapers claiming that we had plagiarized 'Conga' from a Cuban group. 'Conga' went to number one in Cuba, and they could not stand the fact that we had taken a song, a rhythm that was Cuban, and made it so successful and that they had no part in it."

Gloria is not completely comfortable with her role as a symbol of the Cuban exile community, but she did reflect on it at the time of the Pan American Games controversy. "I guess I am a symbol of the fact that culture hasn't died," she reluctantly explained. "And even though we were transplanted, that it's still very much alive in its youth. And we're a symbol to the regime there that's telling them, 'You can't,' 'You're not going to squash us.' Just because you made us leave and because you made life impossible there doesn't mean that our culture is going to disappear."

After that, she chose not to discuss her political views further. She didn't want her role in the exile community to become a recurring theme. "I don't want people to want me to champion their cause," she stated in an interview.

Instead, Gloria has always just hoped to be recognized for her musical talents and for the songs she has taken to the top of the charts. In 1988, her dreams would become reality. She would not only receive support from the public, but she would also be recognized by the industry. And that meant the world to Gloria and the band.

At the American Music Awards, Miami Sound Machine won for Favorite Pop/Rock Group. *Billboard* magazine's 1988 The Year in Music issue awarded Gloria and the band eighteen awards in fourteen categories. They won Top Adult Contemporary Singles and Top Pop Singles for "Can't Stay Away from You," "Anything for You," and "1-2-3"; Top Adult Contemporary Artist; Top Hot Crossover Artist; Top Pop Album Artist; Top Pop Single Artist; Top Pop Album Artist-Duos/ Group; Top Pop Artist of the Year; and Top Pop Singles Producer (Emilio Estefan).

Their hit singles were also played in the movies *Stakeout* ("Rhythm Is Gonna Get You"), *Three Men and a Baby* ("Bad Boy," "Conga"), and *Salsa* ("Mucho Money").

While the world was humming their catchy tunes, Gloria continued performing her show live. A tireless entertainer, she is a true professional onstage. From the moment she appears, her drawing power is enormous. She is attentive to her audience, knowing their pleasure and pandering to it with unabashed delight. Something seems to flow between Gloria and the audience like a transfusion of energy.

Choosing to perform both her English and Spanish hit songs, Gloria remains loyal to *all* her fans. In show after show, she may not be able to define precisely what happens out there under the spotlights but she knows when she has an audience fully on her side. Gloria's *Let It Loose* concert was filled with fun as audiences around the world sang along and danced in the aisles.

Like all great performers, Gloria touches everybody in a different way. She is always conscious of making things work onstage and knows how to move from one emotional plateau to another—immediately, without a break.

As the *Let It Loose* tour wound down, the most exciting night for Gloria Estefan and Miami Sound Machine was yet to come. The final night of the concert brought Gloria home to Miami, where she played before a sell-out crowd of hometown fans, friends, and family in the Miami Arena. The power-packed, throbbing concert was filmed for a special on the Showtime cable channel. It would go on to win three Ace Awards for Best Music Special, Best Directing, and Best Editing. Subsequently, a longer version of the *Homecoming Concert* was released on home video, where it was certified gold in both the U.S. and U.K.

In one segment, Gloria dedicates a new arrangement of "Words Get in the Way" to close friend Julio Iglesias, who was in the audience and who stands to wave to her onstage. Clearly, she has won the admiration of her peers and fellow performers.

Awards, respect, recognition beyond her wildest dreams—all were in the palm of Gloria's hand. She was fully enjoying her life and her success. But not everyone involved with Miami Sound Machine was satisfied. Amid the hoopla surrounding the success of Gloria and the band, the three members of the Jerks remained unimpressed. Problems began with Emilio and the Jerks right after the nominations for the 1988 Grammys were announced. The band had been nominated for Best Vocal Performance by a Duo or Group for the bilingual version of "Anything for You" and Emilio and the Jerks were nominated for Producer of the Year.

What should have been the beginnings of a long association between Emilio and his three coproducers ended on the night of the Grammy Awards telecast. Emilio wanted to sign up Joe Galdo, Lawrence Dermer, and Rafael Vigil for a five-year exclusive contract.

They turned it down, dissatisfied with the lack of recognition they received through two successful albums. "Everybody in the industry thinks that Emilio is the genius behind the whole nine yards," Galdo told a reporter. "People were coming to him to get our sound."

The Jerks were paid a flat fee for their work on *Primitive Love.* They negotiated a better deal for *Let It Loose,* but it still wasn't good enough. They received one half of one point, which amounted to about five cents on every album sold, but the deal also stated Estefan Enterprises would own all their publishing rights. Galdo complains, "I made a couple hundred thousand dollars, but Emilio's made millions."

The last time Emilio saw Galdo was the night of the Grammy awards. "He's Latin, and I'm Latin, and we both have a lot of pride," says Galdo. "If he'd treated us fairly, we would've died for him."

After cutting his ties with Emilio, Joe Galdo was willing to talk about the whole incident. He says he and his partners accepted the original offer because Emilio promised them more money in the end. "He stroked our egos to the max in the studio. He'd come up to me and ask what kind of Rolex I thought Larry would like," says Galdo, who adds that the talk of Rolexes ended when the recording of *Let It Loose* was finished.

According to Galdo, Emilio's input on the *Let It Loose* album, was "he'd come into the studio maybe two, three times a week. Always the same: He'd go over to the engineer and say, 'Sounds great! More percussion, please.' Then he'd ask us what we wanted for dinner, order Cuban food, hang out for an hour or so and disappear."

Even though a studio musician adds to Galdo's story by saying, "As a producer, Emilio Estefan orders a great sandwich in the studio," the facts are there. Emilio has gone on to successfully produce tracks and albums for other performers like Julio Iglesias, Japanese singer Seiko, Barry Manilow, Clarence Clemons—and the list goes on.

Emilio says, "My twelve-year track record as a producer speaks for itself. Twice in the last three years my peers have honored me and my different collaborators with Grammy nominations for Producer of the Year."

Galdo, Dermer, and Vigil weren't the only ones to leave during the *Let It Loose* album. After the tour was over, Kiki Garcia also decided to move on. Though Galdo explains Emilio fired Kiki from the touring band, Garcia hasn't commented on the real reason for his departure. The only thing he has let slip is that Emilio and the new musicians hired from the University of Miami "gave me the vibe that I was just a backup musician. I didn't go eight years to school, and I guess they didn't dig working with me."

Garcia, whose last performance with the band was the night of their homecoming concert in Miami, wanted to leave on a happy note. "On my last night, I asked everybody to sign a band T-shirt, you know, as a souvenir," he says. "I really felt good about having worked with all the guys; they're such great musicians. But when I brought the shirt to Gloria, she got real upset. 'Kiki,' she said, 'you make it sound like we're never going to see each other again.' But we never did."

Most of the band's creative team were out on their own. The Jerks' big project after Miami Sound Machine was the debut album of Bandera, but it didn't set the world on fire. Kiki became involved with writing and producing music for other artists; the latest singer he has worked with is Ana, the bright teen Cuban singer, who also lives in Miami.

As for Gloria and Emilio, they pressed forward with Miami Sound Machine. Band members Jorge Casas and Clay Ostwald became Emilio's new coproducers/arrangers and right-hand men. Immediately following the end of the *Let It Loose* tour, they began planning a new album.

Gloria already had the lion's share of the songs written.

10

The Songwriter

Gloria Estefan's enormous and daringly experimental talents as a songwriter have, undoubtedly, added to her reputation as one of the most versatile performers in music today. When she sits down to compose a new song, it flows out of her like water running out of a well. She never has to force lyrics or the music that shapes her words into a song.

Gifted with a natural instinct and talent, Gloria is generally thought to be one of the industry's best and most prolific composers. The facility that she displays as a songwriter is astounding.

It proves one thing: Gloria really has a way with words. Her songs are written with a perception and directness that have helped her

make a special connection with her fans.
When she sings, she has a distinctive style;
her voice is crystalline: real, urgent, passionate. It is that pure quality of Gloria's voice
that makes it so appropriately suited to the
kinds of songs she sings, be they frenzied, up-
tempo Latin tunes or romantic ballads.

It's interesting to note that even though
Gloria and Emilio are known to have one of
the most solid marriages in show business,
Gloria's songs continuously represent couples
breaking up. Her ballads are generally sad
and grieving, mostly defining lost love. Filled
with rich emotion, they can clutch at the
heart. They definitely reveal a different Gloria from the optimistic and exuberant person
she is onstage or at an interview. Underneath
the superstar veneer, there is the Gloria who
has suffered greatly, and this suffering often
fills her ballads. Any distress she has gone
through in her life is thoroughly and completely worked out through her music. Songwriting is the one great passion in Gloria's
life.

Like any other creative person, Gloria can't
give an explanation for how she writes her
songs. It's simply a case of feeling inspired.
She doesn't analyze or intellectualize it; she
just does it, going with the moment. It's some-

thing that happens, that sort of seizes her. Sometimes she simply thinks of a title. Other times she writes entire songs that remain untitled for a long span of time.

Gloria writes constantly—at home, between taping sessions, in hotel rooms, on the tour bus. The focus of her songs is not necessarily her own life, but rather others' experiences as she has witnessed them. Sometimes when the composing muse fills her mind, Gloria can write many different ideas down and work them out into several songs; she fills pages and pages of notebooks with her rough notations.

It is as a songwriter that Gloria has received the most acclaim, and it is that talent she works hard to refine. Gloria's tunes are natural, sensitive. She has been praised for her sense of melody and her inclusion of rhythm.

Crossing over into American music didn't mean that Gloria would write her songs in Spanish and translate them into English. Both she and the other band members who composed the bulk of Miami Sound Machine's material learned it was much easier to compose the songs in English.

That, according to Gloria, has been "the key to our success. Our ability to actually write—

not translate—our original music and lyrics. We all decided in the beginning that wording in Spanish may not click in English and it sounds tacky to translate. It's best to be able to write songs in English and rewrite them in Spanish."

Producing a Miami Sound Machine album has always been a group effort. All the members, throughout the years, have had the freedom to compose a song, but then have left it up to Emilio to decide what will be recorded and what will be saved for some future date.

"We all write and express our ideas," says Gloria. "Emilio will then come in and suggest certain things. Everybody basically writes what they want, but somebody has to do the picking. At that point, we all sit down and try to decide which are the best songs."

After Emilio makes his decisions, he will play some of the songs for close friends and family to get their opinions on which songs they feel could go on to become hit singles.

For Gloria, creating a new song for a new album can be both rewarding and frustrating, especially when it comes to what Emilio thinks of them. "In English," she says, "he's got the kind of ear that listens for what people understand and what will reach them right away. If I feel strongly about something, he'll see my side, but deep down, whenever he makes a comment, I take it to heart."

Gloria will work on a song for weeks, months even, before she allows Emilio to hear it. When she writes, she sings the words to herself over and over again until she gets the song the way she wants it. Gloria's songs are powerful in their imagery; they have enough depth to be appreciated and enough simplicity to be understood.

In 1988, Gloria Estefan's efforts as a songwriter were applauded by the industry when she won the prestigious BMI award for Songwriter of the Year. While Gloria was recognized as a writer of fine ballads, she also won the award for her work as a collaborator. For example, she and Kiki Garcia proved to be good writing partners when they teamed up to compose "Give It Up," "Rhythm Is Gonna Get You," and "1-2-3" on the *Let It Loose* album. Winning an award for Songwriter of the Year was, without a doubt, one of the highlights in Gloria's career, and it gave her the incentive to continue composing. She always finds time to write a new song, no matter where she is or what she's doing. Her songwriting is her best way of letting her emotions out. The only thing is, she has never had the time to devote herself fully to writing.

She's always composing while traveling. She has often stated that the one thing she would like is a span of time when she could sit down and work full-time on composing.

After the long and tiring *Let It Loose* tour, Gloria announced, "I'm planning a break to relax, go scuba diving, learn to cook, and learn how to play the piano so I can write a lot easier than I do now."

Well, except for relaxing, Gloria did accomplish most of those goals, the most important being that she learned the basics of the piano. This would add a new dimension to her writing and the songs she was about to record for her next album, *Cuts Both Ways*.

11

Cuts Both Ways

"I've written more songs than ever for an album, and I've become more involved in the arranging of some of the songs."

Gloria Estefan was proudly referring to *Cuts Both Ways,* an album she feels is completely hers from top to bottom. When she went in to begin recording the album, Gloria knew she would have to bounce back with a powerful follow-up to the double-platinum *Let It Loose.* But that didn't seem to concern her; she was completely confident with the new collection of songs she and some of the other members of the band had written.

The only difference was that she wanted more of a Latin influence on the new album, and so she decided to take some chances and break some rules. While she was ready to confront her latest material with the same freshness and fervor that originally catapulted her to stardom, Gloria now had new things to say and new ways to say them. She wanted to do a song that would be part pop, part *pure* salsa.

From Emilio, who was completely in favor of testing the waters, she had full encouragement and support. As the band's manager and the album's producer, along with "Sound Machinists" Jorge Casas and Clay Ostwald, Emilio stated, "When you make decisions, you don't make them just for money, you make them more as a career move—as something that will be good for your wife, your child, or other members of the family and the band."

Gloria was fully prepared to begin recording *Cuts Both Ways*. She hoped that when completed, the album would represent the group's history. It was unconsciously in the making for over two years, drawing on their experiences traveling to other countries and playing live performances in those countries.

"The album has our signature Latin high-energy sound," says Gloria, "but it reflects two years of continuously being on the road, where we learned a great deal about our music and ourselves. I had written the songs over a stretch of time . . . wherever inspiration would strike me."

Because "it was recorded in a generally pressure-free atmosphere" at Criteria Studios in Miami, Gloria's creative juices flowed through each and every track. One new aspect of the recording that Gloria felt was ground-breaking was that for the first time both the music track and the vocals were recorded together and not separately as had been done in the past. This "playing live in the studio" created a more natural sound, and, "it's that element people remember," Gloria is also quick to point out. "This album is more of a group effort, in that Emilio coproduced it with two members of the band, and the rest of the group contributed on different levels."

With everyone anxiously awaiting Gloria's new release, CBS Records decided to begin promoting it in the U.S. and to other countries. Even though Gloria Estefan and Miami Sound Machine were now primarily considered an American act, they have never ignored any of their original fans, including their Latin audience. Bunny Freidus says, "The more successful they have gotten, the harder they worked at it." Polly Anthony, vice president of pop promotion for Epic Records, adds, "There's always been a tremendous consideration on Emilio's and Gloria's part toward the Spanish market. Those are their roots. These aren't the kind of people who will ever say good-bye to anyone who has supported them. I know when it comes to copromotions with different radio stations in tour markets, the Spanish station is always right on the list with the Top Forties and ACs." Gloria recorded Spanish versions of two of the album's tracks, "Si Voy a Perderte" ("Don't Wanna Lose You") and "Oye Mi Canto." She also recorded "Here We Are" in Portuguese.

The first hit single off *Cuts Both Ways* was "Don't Wanna Lose You," Gloria's most stirring ballad. The Discos CBS label released the Spanish version of the song at the same time Epic released the English version. Scoring a first for Gloria and the band, it hit number one on both the American and Latin *Billboard* charts simultaneously. The single also reached the top of the charts in Norway, Holland, Finland, England, and Japan.

Cuts Both Ways was met with an overabundance of praise from the moment it was released. And its phenomenal success wasn't limited to the United States or Latin America.

124

The album debuted in the number-one spot in England. It reached the top of the charts in Scotland, Holland, and Belgium and also zoomed to number one in Japan. Its release in England marked the first time a group had two albums reach number one in the same year—*Cuts Both Ways* and *Anything for You* (the retitled *Let It Loose* album). The last band to achieve that kind of success was Abba in 1981.

Gloria's new album and single were universal hits. And that meant it was time for the band to begin another world tour. Gloria and the band were anxious to begin performing the new songs live. A new tour was booked, with the European leg beginning on September 4 and ending on October 22, 1989. In that one-and-a-half-month span, Gloria played to sell-out crowds in England, Scotland, Holland, and Belgium. A true celebrity in Holland, she was asked to leave her footprints in concrete along Amsterdam's Star Boulevard.

Miami Sound Machine mania had certainly built to enormous proportions in Europe. Emilio had been concerned about Gloria and the band's maintaining their success. He was glad he had decided to revamp the new show. Emilio hoped to give the audience something different, not just a copy of the *Let It Loose* tour.

For the new album, Gloria had woven beautiful ballads together. Her songs cast a musical spell on her audience, and it was this approach Emilio wanted for the new show. For one thing, more acoustic instrumentation was added. Emilio wanted to focus more on the music than the glitz. Whereas the *Let It Loose* show had displayed a lot of energy, the new concert focused less on choreography and more on "real serious music," as Emilio put it.

When their engagements in London were announced, 65,000 tickets sold out in less than a week. Gloria Estefan and Miami Sound Machine played to frenzied fans in Sheffield City Hall, Birmingham International Arena, and Edinburgh Playhouse. The highlight of the tour consisted of three nights in London's Wembley Stadium.

Gloria was clearly looking forward to the American leg of her world tour. A route of mostly Eastern states and a few Midwestern states was carefully mapped out. The record company wanted Gloria to tour in the States for two reasons: to promote "Don't Wanna Lose You" and to introduce the second single, "Get On Your Feet," which was just about to be released. Unfortunately, the tour was cut short.

She played some dates in November and December 1989, then caught a bad case of the flu. Suffering from a nasty sore throat, Gloria canceled two Midwestern dates and went to see a specialist. It was then that setback number one occurred for her and the band. The doctor informed her that a blood vessel in her throat had ruptured because of constant coughing.

Luckily, there was no permanent damage. But the doctor warned Gloria that her condition could get worse if she wasn't careful. He prescribed no talking for two weeks and no singing for two months. A worried Emilio immediately announced plans to stop the tour— temporarily. Gloria, who returned home to Miami for a rest, says, "I was really scared. This is my *life.*"

Meanwhile, CBS saw to it that the world kept dancing to the beat of Gloria's music. The album's second single "Get On Your Feet," a moving tune celebrating personal independence, was another hit. A third single, "Oye Mi Canto," also extolled independence, but it seemed a little more risky to release to American audiences. Still, Gloria and Emilio were determined to see it on the charts. "Oye

Mi Canto" is the song Gloria set out to write to prove she could compose pop and salsa and do it successfully. The emotion-filled, semiautobiographical "Oye Mi Canto" confirmed the fact that Gloria had not only crossed over from the Latin market to the Anglo market, but had also earned the right to go back and forth.

Its message is strong, with bold lyrics written by Gloria and a driving Latin rhythm composed by Gloria, Casas, and Ostwald. In the most candid song she has yet written, Gloria is telling the world to break down racial barriers and cast aside prejudice. With racial tension plaguing American cities, Gloria's powerful song seems to say it all. It is a plea for people of all backgrounds to find common ground and unity of purpose.

"Oye Mi Canto" is very special to Gloria Estefan. It's both a tribute to her Latin roots and a message for the entire world to listen to. "I wanted the song to be very Latin," she says. "It was a statement to those critics who see us as just 'watered-down salsa.' And the second part of the song is a celebration of freedom, that you can do what you want to do. It's pure salsa at the end. It goes from one extreme to the other."

She was happy to see it on the charts, but

she says it would never have been accepted five years ago. "Radio wouldn't have touched it with a ten-foot pole," she admits. "But it's definitely opened up since then. All different kinds of music are coming into pop—from rap and hip-hop to heavy metal. I see Latin music as more lasting this time, not just a trend like it was in the thirties. Hopefully, people will be more open to it. Remember, at the beginning no one thought rap music would become part of pop. The same with soul and R and B. But everything is becoming more interwoven and people are listening to more things from other countries. The radio stations have realized this. Hopefully, we've been able to open some doors."

Cuts Both Ways opened up a new world for Gloria Estefan. It was decided that her name would appear on the album's cover alone (you have to look inside at the credits to find Miami Sound Machine). Even though she was still part of the band, she was now regarded as a solo pop female vocalist. When the Grammy Award nominations rolled around, that was exactly the category she was nominated in: Best Female Vocal Performance for "Don't Wanna Lose You." Emilio was nominated for Producer of the Year.

With her throat healing nicely, Gloria decided to make herself visible to television audiences in January and February of the new year, 1990. She signed on as one of four hosts for the seventeenth annual gala American Music Awards. Not only did she appear on one fourth of the live telecast, but she performed "Get On Your Feet" and "Here We Are," another ballad off *Cuts Both Ways* that was beginning to get plenty of radio airplay. Gloria was in top form; it was the first time she had sung in public in two months.

One month later, in February, she performed again at the thirty-second annual Grammy Awards. Dressed in a shiny yellowish-gold strapless dress, Gloria was dazzling both to her peers in the audience of the Shrine Auditorium and to the rest of the world watching the show on television.

Even though she lost the Grammy to Bonnie Raitt, the night's big winner, Gloria smiled and told reporters, "I love her voice and think she's a great songwriter. She deserved it."

Then she added, "I just wish I could have gotten one, too."

Gloria Estefan and Miami Sound Machine weren't without awards, however, having already been cited eleven times in *Billboard* magazine's 1989 The Year in Music issue.

12

Pop's Salsa Songstress and the Magic Man

"When I was shy, I felt I had something in me I wanted to bring out, I just didn't know how to do it," says Gloria Estefan. "It was a painful process, but I forced myself to do it, mostly by watching myself on videotape, which is the most horrendous experience there is. But it's the only time you can see what people are seeing, and if you want to fix it . . ."

In the music business, there are two very important forms of exposure that guarantee the success of an artist's album. One is receiving enough radio airplay; the other is filming videos.

When Epic Records started promoting Gloria and Miami Sound Machine back in the days when American audiences weren't familiar with them, their primary concern was getting them on the radio, on television, and in newspapers. It was very difficult to reach Middle America, because MTV didn't want to play their early videos. But Epic's product manager, Larry Stessel, got Gloria and the band booked on the Johnny Carson show, and they presented awards and performed on the American Music Awards and the Grammys. Having the group appear on shows that so much of America watches was necessary. Feature articles in newspapers like the *Topeka Times* and *Des Moines Register* brought the band the attention they needed in the Midwest.

Still, the key to their success was getting their songs played on radio and their videos played on MTV. It took a little work before both mediums were fully supportive of Gloria and the band. Radio stations were the first to recognize their appeal and played their songs long before they became hits. With *Cuts Both Ways*, the record company distributed excerpts of select cuts to radio stations before the album's official release date. It was the radio music director's job to preview the songs and announce when the album would be in stores.

As for self-promotion, Gloria has always

fully cooperated with radio stations who want interviews. Depending on time, she does one of three things: in-person interviews, telephone interviews, or a new form of promotion that consists of recording answers to scripted questions on a CD. Later they are distributed to local announcers. When the DJ reads the question and plays Gloria's answer, it sounds as if she's in the studio. Says Polly Anthony, vice president of pop promotion for Epic Records, "Until we invent cloning machines we have to think of other options and this has worked very well. It personalizes the whole project."

Gloria's popularity with all age groups can be attributed to the support she's had from radio stations. Larry Stessel says, "I think they've given us a tremendous teen female audience. Adult contemporary radio and VH-1 get all the twenty-one-plus audience, but to get the teenagers you need Top Forty and MTV."

While Miami Sound Machine's early songs were hits on radio, the videos of the same songs only seemed to do well in the Latin community. They couldn't compete on MTV and VH-1. Stessel was responsible for making Gloria's videos more competitive in the market. In order to give them a more contempo-

133

rary look, he hired the best directors in the business.

At the same time, Gloria and Emilio had some ideas that would catch attention. They traveled to Europe and Asia and adopted styles that would become popular months later in America. The change in Gloria's image was also essential. Wearing strapless dresses, black leather, denim or bolero jackets, jeans and short skirts gave her the look of a fresh pop/rock star.

Because each video employs a different director and producer, it is vastly different from the next one. But they all have one thing in common: they show the world what a versatile performer Gloria is. Audiences are very impressed with her dancing ability. Technically, her steps are amazing, especially her ability to pull off fast moves and still make them crystal clear.

In 1990, CBS released a mass-market video cassette of Gloria's greatest hits. Called *Evolution,* it includes thirteen videos, plus four bonuses—Spanish versions of "Anything for You," "Don't Wanna Lose You," and "Oye Mi Canto," and a Portuguese version of "Here We Are."

Even though Gloria admits making videos has never been her favorite part of the business, she has an electric onscreen presence. The nerves she feels during production aren't visible in the finished products. Her most recent videos show a much more mature, self-assured performer. The videos from the *Cuts Both Ways* album, especially the artful black-and-white "Don't Wanna Lose You," and the evocative "Here We Are," are cutting edge. The video for "Oye Mi Canto" won an international MTV award in September 1990.

Which video was the most difficult to film? Without hesitation, Gloria says it was "Can't Stay Away from You." "It was weird to have to touch another man and make it believable," she says. "The guy that did it, it was his first video and in the scene where I pulled him off the couch, we were sweating so badly we slipped out of each other's hands. Afterward, my sister refused to look at me. She walked away, calling me a shameless hussy," Gloria says with a laugh, adding, "Emilio was right there during filming. I told myself I was on the line, I had to do this, and do it right."

If the road to the top has been a long and bumpy one for Gloria Estefan and Miami Sound Machine, their journey up the ladder of success has been cushioned by Emilio Estefan. As the band's personal manager, Emilio proved to be a titan in the industry, a captain of imagination when it came to promoting his talented wife and the band they made famous. His keen eye and sharp mind have been essential to Miami Sound Machine's rise to stardom.

Though Emilio was always involved with the band, it wasn't always completely run by the Estefan family. The decision to keep management in the family was made after they tried an outside manager, unsuccessfully, in 1987.

"We had lots of problems," Emilio recalls. "Things were not done. People tried to contact us and we were never told. Sometimes we would be scheduled to perform and were told that everything would be taken care of—all the lighting and so on. We would arrive and nothing had been done. We'd call the manager and he would hide from us. He wouldn't come to the phone. It was a real pain."

At the time, the *Let It Loose* album wasn't doing well in Europe. "When I fired the manager, our album became number one in England and in Holland," says Emilio. "Our album sales in England were second only to Michael Jackson."

Today, the Estefan family handles almost every aspect of Miami Sound Machine themselves. Emilio is the band's personal manager, group administrator, and producer of albums, while his brother, Jose, acts as manager of MSM's business affairs. Gloria is also largely responsible for most of the group's final decisions. Says Emilio about keeping the business in the family, "We are real secure. It feels ten times better."

Estefan Enterprises is definitely a growing business. They've moved their offices out of Emilio's mother's garage into a two-story building on Bird Road in Miami. Emilio and his brother are currently putting the finishing touches on three state-of-the-art recording studios built in their new office complex, where Emilio will now be able to work on three projects at the same time. The equipment that was installed, which reportedly cost several million dollars, includes a studio for editing.

Several cousins, as well as immediate family members, work in the office. But Emilio works closest with his brother, which he never could have envisioned when the two were growing up. "We used to fight as kids," he says, laughing. "Jose used to hit me a lot. But today, he takes my advice and I respect what he says. We work together well."

Emilio also works well with CBS Records.

Handling most of the band's business on the phone from his spacious office, Emilio admits he has never had any real problems with the label. "Whenever we have a small disagreement, we come to a conclusion and it's always been the right conclusion and the right decision," he explains.

He speaks to the company's president, Tommy Mottola, three or four times a week. "He's like a brother, and so far, he hasn't let me down," says Emilio. "If he has a problem, he tells me and we work it out. When I have a problem, I talk to him and he takes care of it."

Marketing and publicity are provided by the record company. The public relations firm Rogers and Cowan was hired to promote the group in both the American and Spanish markets. The William Morris Agency, one of the largest talent agencies in the world, is in charge of booking concerts for Gloria and Miami Sound Machine worldwide.

The rest is handled by Emilio and his staff at Estefan Enterprises.

Emilio, who had been called "the magic man" by Juan Marcos Avila, one of the band's original members, has certainly lived up to that title. Jorge Pinos, an executive in the international department at the William Morris Agency, says, "I really enjoy working with

Gloria, Emilio, and Miami Sound Machine. They're a very together band. They don't do drugs; they don't drink. Emilio likes to keep everybody happy. He wants a big family. They're very hard workers, they're very loyal, and I respect that a lot."

Today, less effort is placed on publicizing a new Gloria Estefan album and video because the media welcomes her new releases with open arms. Because of the astronomical success of *Let It Loose,* Gloria is now perceived as a general market performer.

"She is beyond regionalization, beyond any ethnic categorization," says Polly Anthony. "She is as credible, as viable, and as valuable to adult contemporary as she is to Top Forty."

By taking chances with her music, Gloria has become a music star of the highest magnitude. And she has Emilio to thank for continuing to support her. Pop's Salsa Songstress and the Magic Man are a dynamite team!

13

The Multiplatinum Life

From nine A.M. to five P.M. every weekday, Gloria and Emilio Estefan are business partners, but when the five o'clock bell rings, they check out of the office and into their marriage.

Gloria and Emilio have one of the healthiest and happiest marriages in show business, mostly due to the fact that success hasn't changed them. "I got lucky with Emilio," Gloria says. "He helps with dishes and loves to clean." They are an incredibly down-to-earth, unpretentious couple who still like to do the same things they did when they were dating. They still eat at the same Cuban restaurants and love to go dancing, especially if their favorite salsa bands are appearing in the Miami Beach dance clubs.

"Gloria and I love to dance to salsa music," confides Emilio. "We rarely get a chance to listen to other people's music, so it's nice." Gloria agrees, adding, "It's great to have someone entertaining *us* for a change."

But while they cling to each other on the dance floor, there is another side to Emilio when the couple dine at restaurants. While she would like their dinners to consist of talking just to each other, she can't keep her husband at their table for long. Emilio, described by Gloria as the social butterfly of the family, always wants to talk with other people.

"Emilio often leaves me alone to order by myself while he table-hops. And I have to fend off the autograph hounds. Sometimes I could just kill that man," Gloria says as her smile turns into laughter.

The fact that they have so many things in common and have shared so many experiences helps to make their marriage a strong one. Being apart is very difficult for both of them. Emilio, who explains how much he misses Gloria when she is on the road traveling without him, says, "I know she really misses me when we're apart—even if it's just for a day or two. But we speak on the phone several times a day when we're not together."

Most important to the Estefans is their close relationship with their families and friends. They laid down permanent roots in Miami, and still see the same people they've known for fifteen years.

"Hey, just because we've made it doesn't mean I'm going to forget who I am and where I come from," asserts Emilio. "Gloria and I still have the same friends we had before we became so popular. We will always be good to our friends. They've always been good to us."

Gloria and Emilio both know when to separate their professional lives from their personal lives. "In every marriage, you have problems," Emilio admits. "I try never to talk about business when I get home. Just family."

Their family includes their son, Nayib, who has had to deal with the fact that his parents are world famous. Gloria and Emilio realize how hard that can be for a child, especially an only child, but Nayib takes it all in stride. The fact that his parents' rise to stardom has been slow and steady has made it easier for him to adjust.

"Most of his friends grew up with him," says Emilio, "and as we've become famous little by little, they see us as human beings instead of as stars. And that's great for him."

Nayib is a spunky, dark-haired, good-looking boy who is showing all signs of wanting to follow in his parents' musical footsteps. That's really no surprise, since he's been surrounded by music all his life. But a few years ago, Nayib went through a period when he wanted to stay home, be a regular kid, and hang out with his friends. All that has since changed. Whenever his mother goes on tour now, Nayib goes, too. Sometimes he wanders onto the stage, staying in the background while Gloria is singing, just to see what it feels like.

"He's a real ham," exclaims Gloria. "We have to drag him off the stage." Both she and Emilio would never discourage their son from having a career in music, but Emilio points out, laughing, "I don't want to manage him. I want to retire someday!"

While Gloria and Emilio are known as "celebrities" in Miami, their fans at home treat them differently from their fans in the rest of the world. "You have to remember that we grew up here in Miami and we spend a lot of time here," declares Emilio. "When we go out, we don't have the same impact that we have in other places in the world—you know, when they see Gloria they go wild. But for us in Miami, although we get approached by lots of people—it's in a nice way, instead of being mobbed."

In some countries, it is necessary for Gloria and Emilio to wear disguises. "We try to hide ourselves a little bit. We use different hats and glasses so that people won't recognize us, but most of the time people realize it's us," says Emilio.

The people of Miami's Latin community have embraced Gloria as a heroine, an immigrant like them, who succeeded in America. They affectionately call her Nuestra Glorita (our Gloria). And the praise they shower her with is obvious whenever she decides to take a stroll down to Little Havana. Gloria often stops at her favorite Cuban restaurant, Casa Lario, for a cup of *café cubano*. It isn't unusual for a crowd of store owners and shoppers to gather to see what the community's biggest star looks like in person. "She makes me cry, she is so beautiful," someone in the crowd says.

Another admirer, holding a freshly signed autograph, comments, "There is no one in the world who means as much to the Cuban people. When she sings, I cry. I am so proud of her."

Gloria seems to be a symbol for a new kind of Latin woman. She is the first to admit that "no Latin man would allow his wife to do what I do. The point is that I'm of the first [Cuban-American] generation that grew up in the United States, and in a way I've had the best of both worlds."

Gloria, who says she doesn't feel Cuban or American, but rather "Latin Miami," seems to have a veritable streak of unpredictability in her. She tends to speak in punch lines. She's very quick when explaining herself, then throws in an afterthought like a curve ball.

"Perhaps it is important to be a Latin woman and not be the stereotypical hot tamale with a lot of makeup and a short red dress," she says, then adds with her trademark smile, "But you might also find me in a short red dress."

Gloria is perpetually smiling. She is sunny and open, and maintains a sense of humor. Everyone who has met Gloria or knows her personally has the same thing to say about her: she is professional, witty and kind, incredibly disciplined, unbelievably determined. Her sister, Becky, describes her as "iron on the outside. When something is bothering her, it doesn't show. I've seen her cry maybe once."

Juan Marcos Avila's wife, Cristina Saralegui, now a talk-show host on a Miami station, says of Gloria, "When you think of entertainers, most people envision an exotic life. But Gloria and Emilio have the most old-fashioned, square marriage. One day, long after Gloria made it big, she came over to take our kids to the beach. No maids, no helpers, just Gloria. She said, 'Look, I've got two hands to spank two little butts, so everybody better behave.' You better believe they listened to her. She's shown you don't have to give up the normal things, like a good husband and family, if you want success."

Gloria is a diva devoid of ego, avoiding the "star treatment" like the plague. She isn't fond of labels being placed on her—even "rock star" makes her feel uncomfortable. After the fame, the awards, the gold and platinum records and achieving every level of success anyone could dream of, what's the downside of Gloria's picture-perfect existence?

What is the toughest part of being a global superstar? For Gloria, traveling has never been easy, but she's learned to tolerate it because she thrives on performing. In fact, she's often said, "Our main thing is to perform. If we could just perform forever—never mind worrying about having hits—that would be great."

The *Let It Loose* tour was a learning experience for Gloria. Not only because it was the first time Emilio didn't go with her, but because she was the only woman (except for her sister Becky) traveling with nine men.

"We travel on a bus with twelve bunks," she said at the time of the tour. "After a hard night of performing and partying, we end up sleeping in our little 'coffins' during the day . . . just like Dracula."

What about when the band checks into a hotel? According to Gloria, that's an entirely different story. With everyone staying in rooms all on the same floor, she has been known to try and get a room on a different floor because she says the party doesn't end for the band members.

Hearing all those doors opening and closing all night, and people coming in and out, made it impossible for Gloria to sleep. "It'd be three in the morning, and I'd peek out and see thirty women wandering around the hallway looking for guys in the band," she explains.

* * *

The most important, and probably most elaborate, thing that Gloria and Emilio did when the money started rolling in was build their dream house. Located on exclusive Star Island, their two-story waterfront estate is breathtaking. They have a thirty-foot speedboat, which they keep anchored at a dock in their backyard on the shore of Miami's Biscayne Bay.

The house was built entirely to the specifications of Gloria and Emilio. They left no stone unturned when deciding what luxuries would be included. The first things to be built inside the house were a sauna and a complete underground recording studio. At the same time, a custom-built racquetball court and saddle-shaped, hand-tiled pool were designed and constructed outside.

When it was complete, the house had everything. The Cuban-style interior design is exquisite: large open rooms with wood ceilings, floors of white coral tiles that flow through the house and onto the poolside terrace. Original paintings by Andy Warhol and Frank Stella hang on the walls; sculptures and exotic plants are placed neatly among the uncluttered furnishings of every room.

However, while the inside of the house is intoxicating, the outside is where Gloria and

Emilio spend a good deal of their time. Sliding glass doors in their elegant bedroom lead them out onto a sun-drenched balcony that overlooks their pool and the blue-green waters of Biscayne Bay. A spiral staircase in the center of the balcony takes them down to the pool terrace.

The one unusual thing Gloria added to the house was an elevator going from the first to second floor. At the time, she said it would come in handy for carrying large equipment up and down, but that wasn't the reason why she put it in.

All her life, Gloria has worried that she would become a burden to her family. She watched it happen to her father and saw what it did to everyone around him. "He was a very athletic, strong, and handsome man," she says. "For years and years, I watched him weaken and die."

So Gloria's mind was temporarily put at ease when the elevator was installed in her home. She wanted to know it was there in case anything ever happened.

14

An Unexpected Setback

The month of March 1990 began on a high note for Gloria Estefan. She was ready to resume the American leg of her world tour, which was sold out everywhere. Leaving her home in Miami, she was happy that Emilio and Nayib would be traveling with her this time. Excitedly, they left for New York City, where the tour would officially take off again at Madison Square Garden.

On March 6, the night before her first concert, Gloria and Miami Sound Machine became the twenty-seventh recording artists in history to receive the CBS International Crystal Globe Award. The awards, which were first conferred in 1974, honor artists whose sales exceed five million outside the United

States. CBS threw a lavish party for Gloria and the band at New York's "21" Club.

The following night, March 7, Gloria rocked Madison Square Garden. Dressed in tight black pants and a fringed jacket, she never looked or sounded better. Her powerful voice filled the Garden and got her audience up out of their seats and dancing to her music. One night later, at New Jersey's Meadowlands Arena, Gloria once again bounced into the spotlight and displayed her enormous energy to the stadium filled with her cheering fans. Unfortunately, those were the only two concerts she would play.

One week later, on March 19, Gloria, Emilio, and Nayib were invited to the White House to meet President George Bush. The day was one of nerves and high emotions. The President talked to Gloria about her recently completed antidrug campaign and posed for photos with her and her family. By the end of the day, Gloria was tired and wanted to rest before her concert in Syracuse the following day.

She and Emilio had been invited to a dinner in New York that same night and though at first she wasn't going to go, she decided to attend. She was glad she did. The Estefans' good friend Julio Iglesias was there, and they spent most of the evening talking to him since they hadn't seen him in a while.

The next morning, Gloria, Emilio, Nayib, two Sound Machine staffers, and Nayib's tutor piled into the customized tour bus rented for the five-hour trip to Syracuse. Emilio had originally mentioned flying so they'd get there more quickly, but Gloria wanted to rest on the bus. When she's had a choice, Gloria has always shied away from air transportation. "If you crash, at least you're not falling thirty-seven thousand feet," she says.

The morning of March 20, 1990, dawned bright and clear. It was a perfect day to be on the road. Nayib was studying his schoolwork at one end of the bus while Emilio was doing business on the phone at the other end. Gloria settled down on one of the bus's two couches in the forward cabin. She put an old spy movie in the video machine, flicked on the TV, and fell asleep.

Around noon, the bus stopped and Gloria awoke. She looked outside and was surprised to see the sun had disappeared, to be replaced by a dark, cloudy sky and a sheet of white snow covering the roads. They were stopped on Interstate 80, near Tobyhanna, Pennsylvania, twenty miles southeast of Scranton. Gloria remembers seeing Emilio standing on the stairwell next to the bus driver, talking on the phone about a truck that had jackknifed in front of the bus. Suddenly there was a loud explosion. The impact knocked Emilio out of his laced tennis shoes and threw Gloria off the couch and onto the floor.

The bus had been struck from behind by a speeding semi, causing it to slam into the truck in front. Gloria watched as the bus driver, Ron "Bear" Jones, leaned over to help Emilio. By doing that, he saved his own life; the spot where he had stood was now a gaping open hole. He was pinned behind the steering wheel, but alive. Emilio and the other passengers all suffered minor injuries.

With the windows all broken and parts of the bus caved in, the snow was coming in as Gloria lay completely still on the floor. She had an electrical taste in her mouth and knew she had broken her back. The pain was just too excruciating. Emilio didn't want to believe it when Gloria told him. He thought maybe her lower back had just given out. She had suffered from a pinched nerve in her back all her life and that had happened before. But she knew the difference in the pain.

Before she began to fight for her life, Gloria worried about Nayib. He was in a completely different section of the bus, and, nervously, she asked Emilio to check on him. If anything had happened to her son, Gloria knew she wouldn't have been able to handle anything. She waited and listened for Emilio, and finally heard him crying. Emilio found Nayib on the floor, clutching his shoulder. He had broken his collarbone, but that was his only injury. Nayib went to comfort Gloria, and held her hand tightly as they waited for help to arrive.

Gloria couldn't believe that what she had been afraid of all her life had actually come to pass. It was the first thought that crossed her mind. To this day she doesn't know how her back was broken. She can only guess that it occurred when she hit two chairs, which had been bolted to the floor next to the couch, but were now both twisted on their sides.

Having Nayib next to her helped keep her spirits up. She was going to fight this; she felt she had to do it, not only for herself, but for her son and the people who loved her. Nayib's tutor, Lori Rooney, said, "Gloria appeared to be in terrible pain. But her only concern was to make sure Nayib thought she was okay."

Gloria slowly tried to lift her legs. There was some movement in both her legs and her feet and she was relieved. "I realized as long as I was able to move my feet even a little, I wasn't going to be paralyzed," she said later.

Having to wait an hour for help to arrive was the worst part. The pain was severe and Gloria wondered how long she'd be able to bear it. A nurse who had been driving on the same road stopped to try and help. When Gloria told her she thought she had broken her back, the nurse ordered her not to move.

Gloria remembered what she had learned in her Lamaze childbirth classes and used it. She picked a spot on the roof of the bus and focused on it to help ease her pain. When the paramedics finally arrived, one asked Gloria's name and when she answered him, he yelled, "Oh my God, we have a celebrity here."

Gloria was strapped onto a board and lifted through the smashed front windshield of the bus. It was the only way out since the bus door was inches from a steep embankment. She was taken to the Community Medical Center Regional Trauma Center in Scranton, arriving at one-thirty P.M., an hour and a half after the accident.

After they took X rays and a CAT scan, and gave Gloria morphine for her pain, Dr. Harry Schmaltz confirmed her earlier fears: she had broken a vertebra in her middle back.

The news of Gloria's broken back was too much for Emilio to handle. When Dr. Schmaltz told him, he fainted. Later, Gloria said, "I think it was the shock of everything. He was maintaining so much control. He kept hoping I was wrong, and when they finally told him that it was true, I think for that moment he just couldn't handle it anymore."

Emilio would say, "I almost lost them both. In a matter of seconds, our whole family was nearly wiped out." He was so worried about Gloria and Nayib that he wasn't examined until a week later, when he found out he had broken a rib and separated his shoulder in the accident. Nayib was treated for his collarbone and given a sling to wear until it was healed.

Gloria was told she had two options in trying to heal the broken vertebra. One was to be put into a body cast for six months, with no guarantee of full recovery; the other was surgery. But the operation didn't come with any guarantees, either. Infection and permanent paralysis were serious things to think about. Gloria decided to have surgery because she wouldn't have to wear a body cast at all.

Next came a series of frantic phone calls. Emilio called everyone they knew, trying to find the right surgeon for this type of operation. Gloria didn't want the doctors in Scranton to feel as if she didn't trust them, but she wanted a specialist. They chose Dr. Michael Neuwirth at the Hospital for Joint Diseases in New York, and the delicate operation was scheduled.

Gloria spent that first night after the accident in a great deal of pain. Medication was kept to a minimum, and she began what she describes as a "horrible cycle of pain and painkillers." She was hooked up to several machines and had tubes running all over her body in case her internal organs shut down because of her broken back.

On the morning of March 21, she was flown by helicopter to New York City. Samy, her close friend and hairdresser, flew from Miami to be with her. "On the way to her operation, I cried with her," he says. "We talked about many things, about how funny it was that this tour just really didn't seem meant to be. First, the tour had to be canceled in December because of the problems with her voice. And now this. Gloria said to me, 'Samy, how life changes from one minute to the next!' "

Two days after the accident, at eight-thirty in the morning, Gloria was prepared for surgery. She remembers Emilio, her family, and

Samy by her side, but after that, the rest is a blur.

When the world came back into focus, Gloria found herself looking up at the white ceiling of the recovery room. She heard her name being called over and over again, and for a moment she thought she was back at the Grammys, with photographers calling her. Instead, Dr. Neuwirth stood over her, trying to wake her up out of the anesthetic. He told her the operation was a success. Gloria looked over at Emilio, who was smiling, and for the first time in two days, she felt she would recover completely.

She was still in pain, but was able to sleep better. The operation itself was a relatively new kind of surgical technique. "I'm very lucky, I think, for it to have happened at the time it did," says Gloria. "Dr. Neuwirth is a great doctor and has been doing a lot of these operations. It could have been a disaster even a couple of years ago."

The operation lasted four hours. During the surgery, Dr. Neuwirth and a team of skilled surgeons inserted two eight-inch metal rods on either side of the broken vertebra. The surgery required bone to be removed from Gloria's pelvis and inserted along the length of the rods. She needed four hundred stitches and the operation left a fourteen-inch scar.

According to Gloria, "The injury was a broken vertebra that pushed into the spine. They had to realign the entire spine. It's kind of like an inside cast, and it'll always be there to keep my spine really strong. They fused six of the vertebrae, two on each side of the injury, so that I wouldn't have any motion there anymore, but thankfully most of the motion is in the pelvic area, so I can move around a lot."

Afterward, Gloria discovered she no longer had the pinched nerve in her lower back that she had had all her life. She jokingly told reporters, "The doctors said, 'What the hell, we'll give her a tune-up as long as we're in there.'" The fact that Gloria was able to maintain a sense of humor is amazing.

Dr. Neuwirth called her a "wonderful patient. There is nothing prima donna-ish about her at all." As for her recovery, he remained optimistic and said, "I don't know if she will be able to do one hundred percent of what she's done before, but I think she'll be able to do substantially the same after six months of recuperation and therapy. Yes, I've seen her videos," he added.

It was almost a miracle that Gloria pulled through her operation in such good shape.

Doctors told reporters that someone in poorer shape might not have been able to withstand the pain and injuries as well and recover as quickly as she did. Of course, the love and support she was receiving from her family, friends, and fans had a lot to do with it. Their prayers and love were constantly with her, and she could take strength in knowing how many people cared so deeply.

Minutes after it happened, Gloria's accident had been picked up by the press. While news bulletins blared across television sets all over the United States, the biggest response came from fans and reporters in Miami. Dr. Steve Greenberg, a medical reporter for Miami's WCIX-TV, said, "I don't think we realized how popular Gloria was in Miami till this."

As the hours dragged on, everyone, it seems, was waiting for word on Gloria's condition. Six South Florida TV stations sent reporters to the crash site. Channel 4 set up a 900 number to record get-well wishes from fans. A crowd gathered outside the band's Miami offices and Miami radio stations began playing her records nonstop. The largest get-well card was made by fans in Fort Lauderdale and the *Miami Herald* ran full-page ads for readers to clip and mail to Gloria.

Miami's Mayor Xavier Suarez, who remembers Gloria from the days she and Miami Sound Machine played at weddings and bar mitzvahs, said, "To see her at the White House made me so proud. Seeing her in the hospital made us all a wreck."

The first report that reached the public was that Gloria might be paralyzed for life, but Dr. Schmaltz in Scranton immediately denied this. He did say that it was very close. "Another half inch of movement of the spine, she'd be completely paralyzed," he explained.

One day after the accident, every newspaper in the country carried stories about Gloria's ordeal and condition. The *Miami Herald* ran the story on its front page for days —until Gloria was safely out of surgery and danger.

During her stay at New York's Hospital for Joint Diseases Orthopaedic Institute, she was deluged with thousands of get-well wishes from fans and her peers in the entertainment industry. Bruce Springsteen, Madonna, Arsenio Hall, Celia Cruz, Jon Bon Jovi, Dick Clark, Guns N' Roses, and Billy Crystal sent flowers; Prince and record producer David Geffen sent CDs; and President Bush called twice. Over 4,000 floral arrangements, 3,000 telegrams, and 48,000 letters and postcards were sent to Gloria. Mary Costello, a hospital spokesperson, said, "It's more than a roomful —we've got a hospital full of flowers. Our auditorium looks like a garden." Gloria later distributed the flowers to other patients and to the AIDS ward at the local VA hospital.

She couldn't believe the response she was receiving. "I didn't know so many people cared," she said. That first night in the hospital, she was watching *The Arsenio Hall Show* and listening to guest Mary Hart tell Arsenio about the accident. Then Arsenio looked into the camera and said, "Gloria, I hope you're feeling better."

"It definitely helped; so many people concentrating positively, praying for me," she says. "It was like an energy I could feel in the hospital. It helped me bear all that pain."

Her road to recovery began immediately, one day after the operation, when she tried raising her head from the pillow. From there, she would do a little more every day until she was able to stand again.

On Wednesday, April 4, just fourteen days after she had been flown to New York and undergone major surgery, Gloria was released from the hospital. Julio Iglesias lent his private plane to her for the trip home to Miami. The press followed her all day, beginning in New York after her official release from the hospital. With Emilio next to her, Gloria held a press conference, obliged the newscasters, and answered all their questions. Then, halfway through the interview, she stood up out of her wheelchair to show how she had recovered and to let everyone know she was feeling well.

She hated the fact that a photo of her strapped to the board and being lifted from the demolished bus was taken and widely circulated in newspapers and magazines. "I didn't want people to see me helpless like that," she said later. For that reason, she decided to walk down the steps of the plane when it landed at Miami International Airport.

Up to that time, Gloria hadn't wanted to look at her back and the fourteen-inch scar the operation left. "I refused to look at it," she says. "I saw it by mistake in Julio Iglesias's plane. I had to go to the bathroom, and he's got mirrors all around! 'Damn,' I thought, 'there it is.' I got curious and looked and then I got depressed. But it's healing really well. The plastic surgeon who closed me up said he was getting religious after my accident. He said that the way my spine was mauled, I shouldn't be able to move."

Samy would later reveal that Gloria was in

pain during the entire flight home from New York to Miami. "In the jet, they had to give her painkillers, but when she arrived in Miami, you'd never know she was hurting. She's a trooper."

Whatever Gloria was feeling that day didn't show as she spoke to her fans at a podium on the airport runway. From the window before landing, she could see the two hundred people waiting for her arrival and she wasn't going to disappoint them. Among the people who had gathered and waited for an hour were members of the Gloria Estefan Fan Club, local TV and radio stations, her son Nayib, and members of her extended family.

Lily Estefan, Emilio's niece, talked about the trauma the family had been going through since Gloria's accident. "We've all been going crazy. Emilio is *sooo* tired," she said. Waiting for the plane to arrive, Lily watched over Nayib, who was playing with his Teenage Mutant Ninja Turtle dolls on the roof of Emilio's black and silver Rolls-Royce.

When the white jet plane finally landed and the hatch opened, Nayib, Lily, and Emilio's aunt Hortencia ran up to greet Gloria. The crowd waited. For two long minutes, no one came down. Then Gloria climbed slowly down the stairs, accompanied by Emilio, who held her arm with a tight grip.

She stood at the podium and spoke in a soft voice. "I want you to know I've felt every one of your prayers from the very first moment," she said to the cheering crowd. She proceeded to "thank Emilio for waiting to faint until I got to the hospital." She acknowledged her son, her family, her hairdresser Samy, and Julio Iglesias. A smile broke out on her pale face as she mentioned the metal rods implanted in her back. "I hope I don't ring all the time now when I go through those things at airports," she said. Then, seriously, she confided, "I will work as hard as I can to come back."

Gloria's therapy began immediately after returning to her home in Miami. Three days a week, from eleven A.M. to five P.M., she worked out with her personal trainer. She started slowly with swimming and the stationary bicycle. The weights and aerobics would come much later. The exercises were to strengthen her arms and legs. To speed her recovery, she saw a therapist who uses massage.

For the most part, Gloria's recovery has progressed very well. But even though she was looking terrific on the outside, she continued to suffer from pain. The crash had short-circuited her central nervous system and she was still feeling occasional shocks. Some areas of skin on her legs remained hypersensitive, and at night, pain jarred her awake every forty-five minutes. She depended on Emilio for everything. Little things like walking, bending over the sink to wash her face, putting on her clothes, became impossible chores. She had to learn how to do everything all over again. Each day became a new triumph for her.

The accident proved how strong Gloria and Emilio's marriage is. In the hospital, nurses told her that some marriages break up at a time of crisis. "They agreed that when there's no real love in a relationship, hardship tends to separate you rather than bring you closer together," says Gloria. "The healthy one loses patience. When this happened, Emilio showed me how much he really loves me. He was there every second for me. I tell him, 'I hope I never have to show you the way you've shown me.'"

Not long after coming home, Emilio gave Gloria a pair of dalmatian puppies born on March 22, the day of her operation. He named them Ricky and Lucy after the other famous Cuban-American musician and his superstar wife. Emilio would keep Gloria laughing by joking with her, but he openly admitted that her suffering was killing him inside.

A multimillion dollar lawsuit was filed against the driver and owners of the truck that hit them, but Emilio says, "No amount of money can make up for what Gloria has gone through."

When times got rough during her recovery, Gloria stayed optimistic, sometimes wincing in pain during workouts, but never complaining. The success story of 49er quarterback Joe Montana was very encouraging. "He had a horrible back injury and came back to set records," says Gloria, who is a big football fan.

The most difficult thing for Gloria was getting used to the fact that permanent metal rods were implanted in her back. After the operation, she was given her post-op X rays, which showed the rods and the steel clamps gripping her spinal column. But she says, "I try not to think about them. I used to think I saw them in the mirror, jutting out, but it was in my mind. Emilio calls me Robocop because of all my high-tech replacement parts. But I told him he should call me Robopop instead."

As Gloria began regaining her strength, she

reevaluated her life. So much had happened. And so much had *almost* happened. She knew it would take months for the bones to fuse. Even though she announced her main goal was to return to the stage and be better than ever, she remained realistic.

"I'm very fortunate that the break happened at the waist, so I'll be able to bend my back and dance," she said, then added, "I just feel very lucky to be alive and to be able to walk again."

15

Starting Over

Gloria's recovery has been nothing short of miraculous, but the accident and her ordeal getting through it have made her take another look at her life; where she is going, what she wants out of it, and what is most important to her.

During her convalescence, Gloria thought long and hard about her next step, both personally and professionally. With music remaining her top priority, she began writing new songs for her next album, *Into the Light.*

"You have to be careful what you ask for because I had always said I'd really like time to write, and I have it now, boy," Gloria told *Good Morning America* in May 1990. She took full advantage of the time she was forced to take off by using it wisely. Each day seemed to be better than the last. Her pain had lessened; she successfully passed the physical therapy stage and was in the serious workout stage of her recovery in less time than originally anticipated. Things were looking up for Gloria.

The emotions she felt from day to day helped her put words and music down on paper. The accident had certainly given her a new perspective on life and she was going to write it all down. "Sometimes the most beautiful songs come out of the worst experiences," she explained. "And even though I'm not going to turn this into a whole album, some songs are probably going to have a lot of the feelings that I've felt and feelings I've gotten from other people."

Meanwhile, with her career in limbo, CBS continued releasing singles off her *Cuts Both Ways* album. "Here We Are" topped the charts the week of her accident while the title track, "Cuts Both Ways" inched its way up *Billboard*'s Hot 100 chart in July. On July 28, it became Gloria's sixth number-one hit on the Hot Adult Contemporary Chart.

CBS Discos also released *Exitos de Gloria Estefan*, a package of her greatest hits, recorded in Spanish. Gloria considers it her gift to the Latin community and those who supported her and Miami Sound Machine throughout their fifteen years together.

"We've never thought of abandoning Spanish for one minute," says Gloria. "We will always record in Spanish. We're Latin Americans; Spanish is our mother language. Like I said, it's our roots—we're proud of our heritage."

A newly recorded version of her Spanish hit "Renacer" was added to the hit parade lists of many stations in the U.S. and Puerto Rico only two weeks after its release in October 1990.

Gloria herself was back in the public eye by May, but she wasn't able to perform yet. One of her first public outings was attending Taylor Dayne's concert at the Sunrise Theater outside Miami. Backstage, she posed with Taylor and another guest, Ann Corliss of Exposé. Also in May, Gloria received an award on *Aplauso 92,* a variety special that was broadcast on a Spanish TV station. She spoke on the show, but did not sing. On September 12, 1990, at Columbia Sound Stage 15 in Culver City, California, Gloria presented CBS president Tommy Mottola with the Spirit of

Life Award for his work with the City of Hope Organization. Gloria told reporters, "I'm really proud to give this award to him. It's wonderful to be back and healthy."

Music, undoubtedly, remains Gloria's first love, and she doesn't know if she'll ever desert it for another career. If she wants to, she can tackle any area of the entertainment industry. Something that is constantly mentioned is movies. Many producers have voiced an interest in moving Gloria out of the recording studio and into the movie studio. There have been numerous scripts submitted for her consideration but she's rejected all of them. She isn't really sure she wants to make a movie.

Three years ago, she rejected the idea completely by saying, "I don't feel like an actress. It would take a lot of time I don't have now. I'm a singer; that's what I love to do. Acting would take too much of my energy."

The bottom line is that while scripts have been sent to Gloria, nothing has been good enough for her to commit to. "If I were to try acting, it would have to be for a very special project," she says. "Believe me, some of the scripts I've been sent are pretty awful! I mean, I have *no* desire to play a vampire!"

Jorge Pinos of the William Morris Agency says a musical would be perfect for Gloria, and she agrees. That would be the only type of movie that would lure her temporarily away from her music career.

CBS president Tommy Mottola sees her as an artist with unlimited potential and envisions a bright future for her. "When you have a mass-appeal artist with a strong Latin base who writes and sings her own songs, there's no limit to what you can do and how long you can do it," he says. "With Gloria, that might mean a combination of films and Broadway. We can use all of those areas to be a parallel and an adjunct when we see that we're ready to take the next step."

After her next tour is finished, Gloria plans on taking time off to have another baby. "Emilio would love to have a little girl," she says. "But we'd both be happy with a son or a daughter, as long as it was healthy. I want to make sure our baby has every chance."

With so much to look forward to, Gloria has many things on her list yet to accomplish. As she stated when *Cuts Both Ways* was released, "We have no plans to stop growing. Trust me, we're very greedy in that respect."

Having already been in the eye of a hurricane that would have wiped out others, Gloria Estefan emerged from it, washing away the rain and forging ahead stronger than ever. She is ready for all the challenges her future will bring.

Discography

American Albums

Miami Sound Machine—*Eyes of Innocence* (1984)

Tracks

- "Dr. Beat" (Music and lyrics by Enrique E. Garcia)

- "Prisoner of Love" (Music and lyrics by Enrique E. Garcia)

- "OK" (Music and lyrics by Wesley B. Wright)

- "Love Me" (Music and lyrics by Gloria M. Estefan)

- "Orange Express" (Music by S. Watanabe, lyrics by Wesley B. Wright)

- "I Need a Man" (Music and lyrics by Enrique E. Garcia)

- "Eyes of Innocence" (Music and lyrics by Gustavo Lezcano)

- "When Someone Comes into Your Life" (Music and lyrics by Gloria M. Estefan)

- "I Need Your Love" (Music and lyrics by Enrique E. Garcia)

- "Do You Want to Dance" (Music and lyrics by Enrique E. Garcia)

Miami Sound Machine - Primitive Love (1985)

Tracks

- "Body To Body" (Music and lyrics by Suzi Carr, Lawrence Dermer, Joe Galdo)

- "Primitive Love" (Music and lyrics by Lawrence Dermer, Joe Galdo, Rafael Vigil)

- "Words Get in the Way" (Music and lyrics by Gloria M. Estefan)

- "Bad Boy" (Music and lyrics by Lawrence Dermer, Joe Galdo, Rafael Vigil)

- "Falling in Love (Uh-Oh)" (Music and

lyrics by Lawrence Dermer, Joe Galdo, Rafael Vigil)

- "Conga" (Music and lyrics by Enrique E. Garcia)

- "Mucho Money" (Music and lyrics by Lawrence Dermer, Joe Galdo, Rafael Vigil)

- "You Made a Fool of Me" (Music and lyrics by Wesley B. Wright)

- "Movies" (Music and lyrics by Lawrence Dermer, Joe Galdo, Rafael Vigil)

- "Surrender Paradise" (Music and lyrics by Suzi Carr, Lawrence Dermer, Joe Galdo)

Gloria Estefan and Miami Sound Machine
—*Let It Loose* (1987)

Tracks

- "Betcha Say That" (Music and lyrics by Joe Galdo, Lawrence Dermer, Rafael Vigil)

- "Let It Loose" (Music and lyrics by Lawrence Dermer, Joe Galdo, Rafael Vigil)

- "Can't Stay Away from You" (Music and lyrics by Gloria M. Estefan)

- "Give It Up" (Music and lyrics by Gloria M. Estefan, Enrique Garcia, Randall Barlow)

- "Surrender" (Music and lyrics by Joe Galdo, Lawrence Dermer, Rafael Vigil)

- "Rhythm Is Gonna Get You" (Music and lyrics by Gloria M. Estefan and Enrique Garcia)

- "Love Toy" (Music and lyrics by Lawrence Dermer, Joe Galdo, Rafael Vigil)

- "I Want You So Bad" (Music and lyrics by Lawrence Dermer, Joe Galdo, Rafael Vigil)

- "1-2-3" (Music and lyrics by Gloria M. Estefan and Enrique Garcia)

- "Anything for You" (Music and lyrics by Gloria M. Estefan)

Gloria Estefan—*Cuts Both Ways* (1989)

Tracks

- "Ay, Ay, I" (Music and lyrics by Gloria Estefan; arranged by Gloria Estefan, Jorge Casas, Clay Ostwald)

- "Here We Are" (Music and lyrics by Gloria Estefan; arranged by Gloria Estefan, Jorge Casas, Clay Ostwald)

- "Say" (Music by Jon Secada, Bill Duncan; lyrics by Jon Secada; arranged by Jorge Casas, Clay Ostwald)

- "Think About You Now" (Music and lyrics by Jorge Casas; arranged by Jorge Casas and Clay Ostwald)

- "Nothin' New" (Music and lyrics by Gloria Estefan; arranged by John Haag, Tom McWilliams, Scott Shapiro, Gloria Estefan, Jorge Casas, Clay Ostwald)

- "Oye Mi Canto" (Hear My Voice) (Music by Gloria Estefan, Jorge Casas, Clay Ostwald; lyrics by Gloria Estefan; arranged by Gloria Estefan, Jorge Casas, Clay Ostwald)

- "Don't Wanna Lose You" (Music and lyrics by Gloria Estefan; arranged by Gloria Estefan, Jorge Casas, Clay Ostwald)

- "Get On Your Feet" (Music by John De Faria, Jorge Casas, Clay Ostwald; lyrics by John De Faria; arranged by John De Faria, Jorge Casas, Clay Ostwald)

- "Your Love Is Bad for Me" (Music and lyrics by Gloria Estefan; arranged by John Haag, Tom McWilliams, Jorge Casas, Clay Ostwald)

- "Cuts Both Ways" (Music and lyrics by Gloria Estefan; arranged by John De Faria, Jorge Casas, Clay Ostwald)

(CD and cassette include two bonus tracks "Oye Mi Canto" (Spanish version) and "Si Voy a Perderte" (Spanish version of "Don't Wanna Lose You"))

Gloria Estefan—Into the Light (1991)

Tracks

- "Coming Out Of The Dark" (Music and lyrics by Gloria Estefan, Emilio Estefan, John Secada)

- "Seal Our Fate" (Music and lyrics by Gloria Estefan)

- "What Goes Around" (Music and lyrics by Clay Ostwald, Jorge Cassas, John Secada)

- "Nayib's Song (I Am Here For You)" (Music and lyrics by Gloria Estefan)

- "Remember Me With Love" (Music and lyrics by Gloria Estefan)

- "Heart With Your Name On It" (Music and lyrics by Diane Warren)

- "Sex in the '90s" (Music and lyrics by Gloria Estefan)

- "Close My Eyes" (Music and lyrics by Gloria Estefan)

- "Light Of Love" (Music and lyrics by John Secada and Randy Barlow)

- "Live For Loving You" (Music and lyrics by Gloria Estefan, Emilio Estefan, Diane Warren)

- "Mama Yo Can't Go" (Music and lyrics by

John Secada, Tom McWilliams, Scott Shapiro)

- "Desde La Oscuridad" ("Coming Out Of The Dark"—Spanish version)

Spanish Albums

In 1976, Miami Sound Machine recorded its first of two albums for a local Miami record label. Two more albums were released on their own label. Between the years 1981–1983, they recorded four Spanish-language albums for Discos CBS International, the Miami-based Hispanic division of CBS Records.

Exitos de Gloria Estefan (Greatest Hits in Spanish) (1990)

Tracks

- "Renacer" (Music and lyrics by Oliva, Giordano, Serrano, Murciano)

- "Conga" (Music and lyrics by Enrique Garcia)

- "No Sera Facil" (Music and lyrics by Gloria Estefan)

- "Dr. Beat" (Music and lyrics by Enrique Garcia)

- "Regresa a Mi" (Music and lyrics by Enrique Garcia)

- "No Te Olvidare" (Music and lyrics by Gloria Estefan)

- "Dingui-Li-Bangue" (Spanish version by Gloria Estefan; original version by J. D. San and Mac Donys)

- "No Me Vuelvo a Enamorar" (Music and lyrics by Gloria Estefan)

- "Si Voy a Perderte" (Music and lyrics by Gloria Estefan; special mix by Humberto Gatica)

- "Oye Mi Canto" (Music and lyrics by Gloria Estefan)

- "Here We Are" (Portuguese version) (Music and lyrics by Gloria Estefan)

Other Projects

Goya . . . a life in song (1989). This album contains an introductory selection of songs from a forthcoming stage musical. Written by Maury Yeston and produced by Phil Ramone, the singers appearing on the album are Placido Domingo, Dionne Warwick, Seiko, and Richie Havens. Gloria sings "Picture It" with Joseph Cerisano and "Hasta Amarte" (Till I Loved You) with Placido Domingo. Spanish adaptation on the latter is by Gloria.

Gloria Estefan and Miami Sound Machine's music has also been used in the following hit films:

- *Top Gun* ("Hot Summer Nights")

- *Stakeout* ("Rhythm Is Gonna Get You")

- *Cobra* ("Suave")

- *Three Men and a Baby* ("Bad Boy," "Conga")

- *Salsa* ("Mucho Money")

Videography

Gloria Estefan and Miami Sound Machine Homecoming Concert (1989)

The triumphant final concert of the *Let It Loose* tour performed before a SRO crowd of fans at the Miami Arena. The concert was filmed for the Showtime cable channel and won three ACE awards for Best Music Special, Best Directing, and Best Editing. Producer: Paul Flattery; director: Jim Yukich; audio producer: Emilio Estefan, Jr.; recorded and mixed by Eric Schilling. Running time: 80 minutes.

Songs: Hot Summer Nights, Bad Boy, Surrender Paradise, Can't Stay Away from You, Let It Loose, Baila Conmigo/A Toda Maquina/Dingui-Li-Bangue (medley), Falling in Love (Uh-Oh), Words Get in the Way, No Sera Facil/Me Enamore/Renacer (medley), 1-2-3, Rhythm Is Gonna Get You, Conga, Betcha Say That, Dr. Beat, Anything for You

Gloria Estefan and Miami Sound Machine— Evolution (1990)

Seventeen smash videos chronicle the evolution of Gloria's rise to international stardom.

Executive producer: Emilio Estefan, Jr. Running time: 74 minutes.

Songs: Conga, Dr. Beat, Bad Boy, Words Get in the Way (live), Rhythm Is Gonna Get You, Betcha Say That, Can't Stay Away from You, Anything for You, 1-2-3, Don't Wanna Lose You, Get On Your Feet, Here We Are, Oye Mi Canto (Hear My Voice). Plus four bonus videos: No Te Olvidare (Anything For You—Spanish version), Si Voy a Perderte (Don't Wanna Lose You—Spanish version), Toda Pra Voce (Here We Are—Portuguese version), Oye Mi Canto (Spanish version)

About the Author

Grace Catalano is the author of two consecutive *New York Times* best-sellers: *New Kids on the Block* (Bantam) and *New Kids on the Block Scrapbook* (NAL/Signet). Her other books include *Paula Abdul: Forever Yours, Kirk Cameron: Dream Guy, River Phoenix: Hero and Heartthrob, Alyssa Milano: She's the Boss, Teen Star Yearbook, Richard Grieco: Hot 'n' Cool,* and *Fred Savage: Totally Awesome.* Grace is currently the editor of the entertainment magazines *Dream Guys* and *Dream Guys Presents.* She and her brother, Joseph, wrote and designed *Elvis: A 10th Anniversary Tribute* and *Elvis and Priscilla.* Grace lives on the North Shore of Long Island.

Famous Lives

from St. Martin's Paperbacks

LIBERACE: THE TRUE STORY
Bob Thomas
_____ 91352-4 $3.95 U.S.   _____ 91354-0 $4.95 Can.

THE FITZGERALDS AND THE KENNEDYS
Doris Kearns Goodwin
_____ 90933-0 $5.95 U.S.   _____ 90934-9 $6.95 Can.

CAROLINE AND STEPHANIE
Susan Crimp and Patricia Burstein
_____ 91116-5 $3.50 U.S.   _____ 91117-3 $4.50 Can.

PATRICK SWAYZE
Mitchell Krugel
_____ 91449-0 $3.50 U.S.   _____ 91450-4 $4.50 Can.

YOUR CHEATIN' HEART:
A BIOGRAPHY OF HANK WILLIAMS
Chet Flippo
_____ 91400-8 $3.95 U.S.   _____ 91401-6 $4.95 Can.

WHO'S SORRY NOW?
Connie Francis
_____ 90386-3 $3.95 U.S.   _____ 90383-9 $4.95 Can.

Publishers Book and Audio Mailing Service
P.O. Box 120159, Staten Island, NY 10312-0004

Please send me the book(s) I have checked above. I am enclosing $_____
(please add $1.25 for the first book, and $.25 for each additional book to
cover postage and handling. Send check or money order only—no CODs) or
charge my VISA, MASTERCARD or AMERICAN EXPRESS card.

Card number _____

Expiration date _____ Signature_____

Name _____

Address _____

City _____ State/Zip _____

Please allow six weeks for delivery. Prices subject to change without notice.
Payment in U.S. funds only. New York residents add applicable sales tax.

FL 1/89